Normal Adolescence

❧❧ Formulated by the

Committee on Adolescence

GROUP FOR THE ADVANCEMENT OF PSYCHIATRY

Normal Adolescence:

ITS DYNAMICS AND IMPACT

NEW YORK ❧ CHARLES SCRIBNER'S SONS

This book is dedicated to the memory of Joseph J. Michaels, M.D., our beloved colleague and fellow committee member, who worked with us in the formulation of the book but whose death prevented him from seeing it reach publication.

1113151719 C/P 201816141210
791113151719 C/C 2018161412108

Printed in the United States of America
Library of Congress Catalog Card Number 68–12511

SBN 684–10199–8 (trade cloth)
SBN 684–71781–6 (trade paper, SL)

Statement of Purpose

The Group for the Advancement of Psychiatry has a membership of approximately 185 psychiatrists, organized in the form of a number of working committees that direct their efforts toward the study of various aspects of psychiatry and toward the application of this knowledge to the fields of mental health and human relations.

Collaboration with specialists in other disciplines has been and is one of GAP's working principles. Since the formation of GAP in 1946 its members have worked closely with such other specialists as anthropologists, biologists, economists, statisticians, educators, lawyers, nurses, psychologists, sociologists, social workers, and experts in mass communication, philosophy, and semantics. GAP envisages a continuing program of work according to the following aims:

1. To collect and appraise significant data in the field of psychiatry, mental health, and human relations;
2. To re-evaluate old concepts and to develop and test new ones;
3. To apply the knowledge thus obtained for the promotion of mental health and good human relations.

GAP is an independent group and its reports represent the composite findings and opinions of its members only, guided by its many consultants.

Normal Adolescence: Its Dynamics and Impact was formulated by the Committee on Adolescence, whose members are listed at the end of the Preface. Members of all other committees are listed in Appendix B.

I see no hope for the future of our people if they are dependent on the frivolous youth of today, for certainly all youth are reckless beyond words. . . . When I was a boy, we were taught to be discreet and respectful of elders, but the present youth are exceedingly wise and impatient of restraint.

HESIOD: EIGHTH CENTURY B.C.

Preface

From the beginning of recorded history there are references to youth which suggest that adults characteristically view adolescents with considerable ambivalence. Attitudes range from approval and frank admiration, through a kind of amused and sometimes anxious tolerance, to concern, apprehension, dismay, and even angry condemnation. Any one of these attitudes may be directed toward a particular adolescent or group of adolescents; all of them are likely to be directed toward any adolescent at different times as he progresses through this stage of human development. More often than not, and certainly this is currently true, the expressed attitudes of adults about adolescents tend to be negative and take the form of severe criticisms, dire predictions, and sweeping generalizations leveled at them not so much as individuals but as a generation that poses a threat to the existing social order. Nevertheless, each successive adult generation and society somehow survive the presumed threat posed by adolescents.

It is of interest to note, also, that the adult's experience of having been an adolescent usually is of little or no value in aiding him to understand those who now are the adolescents. It is today's adolescents who tomorrow, from their position as the new adult generation, will express the same kinds of concerns about adolescents as were only recently expressed about them. This, too, seems to be an inevitable and therefore presumably normal condition in human relationships.

Yet we of the Committee on Adolescence question whether the fact that adolescence normally is a troubled and stressful time of life characterized by questioning and rebelling against the rules and values of

7

society means that nothing can be done to alleviate the conflict between adolescent and society. We think it is of vital importance that adolescence be seen as a constructive stage in human development, both for the individual adolescent and for society. It is our hope that this presentation of the psychodynamics of normal adolescence will illuminate the transition from childhood to adulthood and increase the understanding and rapport between the adolescent and adult generations.

Our approach to the subject of normal adolescence is comprehensive, embracing the three determinants which are universal for any stage of individual human development, namely, biology, culture, and psychology. On the other hand, as comprehensive as this book is, it still is by no means an exhaustive treatise.

The chapter on biology presents a brief review of the all-important physical and physiologic changes of puberty, at the same time taking special note of the impact of puberty on the child and his psychological development. The chapter on cultural factors seeks to give an appreciation both of the kinds of socio-cultural forces which come to bear on the adolescent, and of the influence of the developing adolescent on his family and his own subcultural or societal group. Both the cross-cultural comparisons and the examples from subcultural groups in our own society are necessarily limited in number, and are selected to serve the purposes of illustration. The chapter on psychology discusses the emotional, intellectual, and psychological development and functioning of the adolescent as he progresses through this stage of transition from childhood to adulthood.

Certain important considerations have contributed to the orientation and content of this report. (1) In our attempt to understand and formulate the psychodynamics of normal adolescence we have employed the concepts and insights of psychoanalytic psychology, as validated by our own clinical and nonclinical observations and experience. To us, it is the most comprehensive psychology of the human being, and it allows for the most adequate explanations and formulations of development and behavior. (2) As psychiatrists and psychoanalysts, we are accustomed to working primarily with adolescents who are in trouble with themselves or others. On the one hand, this fact requires us to be continuously concerned with the question of what is normal adolescence, but, on the other hand, it may somewhat distort our view of normality. (3) Adolescent development takes place within a given cultural context, and this report undoubtedly bears the imprint, the shadings, the bias of our particular culture, and especially so of the middle- and upper-middle-class culture with which we are most familiar.

Both the Committee on Adolescence and this book, in large measure, owe their existence to the efforts of Edward J. Hornick, M.D., the first chairman of the Committee, and it is with fondness and much appreciation that we call attention to his contribution.

We also wish to acknowledge the special contribution of Weston La Barre, Ph.D., Professor of Anthropology at Duke University, who functioned both as a most valued consultant and as a regular member of the Committee.

During the early stages of discussion and formulation of this book the Committee had the benefit of the thinking of former Committee members Helen Carlson and Mabel Ross, and of Silvio J. Onesti, GAP Fellow.

We are indebted also to a number of individuals outside of GAP, who accepted our invitation to read and criticize the manuscript of this book, from the vantage point of their varying professional backgrounds: R. Freed Bales, Ph.D., Professor of Social Relations, Harvard University; Kenneth G. Chinburg, M.D., Private Practice of Psychiatry, Denver; Rose L. Coser, Ph.D., Associate Sociologist, McLean Hospital, Belmont, Massachusetts; John F. Crigler, Jr., M.D., Assistant Professor of Pediatrics, Children's Hospital, Boston; Ronald B. Feldman, M.D., Director of Family Psychiatry, Jewish General Hospital, Montreal; Robert J. Gaukler, M.D., Faculty, Philadelphia Psychoanalytic Institute; George W. Goethals, Ed.D., Lecturer on Social Relations, Harvard University; Edward E. Hunt, Jr., Ph.D., Professor of Anthropology, Hunter College; George C. Ham, M.D., Private Practice of Psychiatry, Chapel Hill, North Carolina; Waldo E. Nelson, M.D., Editor, *Textbook of Pediatrics;* David Riesman, D.C.L., L.H.D., Henry Ford II Professor of Social Sciences, Harvard University; John M. Rhoads, M.D., Professor of Psychiatry, Duke University

9

Medical Center; Irene Pierce Stiver, Ph.D., Chief Psychologist, Mc-Lean Hospital, Belmont, Massachusetts.

The Committee is grateful to the Morris and Sophie Kardon Foundation of Philadelphia for its generous financial support to the editorial and secretarial services required in the readying of this book. We also wish to express our appreciation to Lester Kardon for reading and criticizing the manuscript from the layman's point of view.

For her services in the preparation of the manuscript, the Committee expresses its thanks to Nancy Lonsinger.

In preparing this book we have endeavored to produce a coherent and integrated blending of our own ideas with those of others, and have acknowledged sources only in the Bibliography, not in the text. This latter fact should not be construed as a lack of awareness on our part of our indebtedness to those so acknowledged.

COMMITTEE ON ADOLESCENCE
GROUP FOR THE ADVANCEMENT OF PSYCHIATRY

Calvin F. Settlage, Chairman
Warren J. Gadpaille
Mary O'Neil Hawkins
Joseph D. Noshpitz
Vivian Rakoff
Henry Wermer

Contents

INTRODUCTION   17

CHAPTER 1
THE BIOLOGY OF ADOLESCENCE   19

    The Complex Changes of Puberty   20
    Responses of Adolescents to Puberty   22
    Psychological and Social Aspects of Puberty   24

CHAPTER 2
CULTURAL FACTORS IN ADOLESCENCE   27

    Criteria of Adulthood   28
    Culture as "Environment" in Adolescence   29
    Western Culture as Environment in
      Adolescence   32
    Universal Tasks of Adolescence   34
    Cultural Facilitation and Inhibition at
      Adolescence   35
    Adolescence in the American Middle Class   38
    Discontinuity of Role from Childhood to
      Adulthood   44
    Rapid Social Change as a Problem of
      Adolescence   48

CHAPTER 3
THE PSYCHOLOGY OF ADOLESCENCE   50

    The Role of Childhood Experience   *51*
    Preadolescence   *55*
    The Beginning and Ending of Adolescence   *59*
        THE ONSET   *59*
        THE PHASES   *59*
        THE OFFSET   *62*
    Early Adolescence   *63*
        THE IMPACT OF PUBERTY   *64*
        THE MOVE TOWARD INDEPENDENCE   *65*
        THE PEER GROUP   *68*
        MASTURBATION   *70*
        MENSTRUATION   *73*
        THE NEW BODY AND SELF IMAGE   *74*
        ACTION AND IMPULSIVE BEHAVIOR   *75*
        THE CAPACITY FOR THOUGHT   *76*
        BOY-GIRL RELATIONSHIPS   *77*
        THE RESOLUTION OF EARLY ADOLESCENCE   *78*
        MAJOR CHARACTERISTICS OF EARLY
        ADOLESCENCE   *79*
    Late Adolescence   *80*
        ADOLESCENT LOVE AND THE ROLE OF
        COITUS   *85*
        IDENTITY SEEKING AND IDEALISM   *88*
        IDENTITY AND OCCUPATIONAL CHOICE   *90*
        ATTAINMENT OF ADULT PREROGATIVES   *91*
        THE RESOLUTION OF ADOLESCENCE   *93*

CHAPTER 4
DYNAMICS OF ADULT RESPONSES
TO ADOLESCENCE   95

CONCLUSION   100

CONTENTS

APPENDIX A   105

    Endocrinology of Adolescence   *105*

    Sequence of Pubertal Phenomena   *108*

        GENITAL DEVELOPMENT IN MALES   *108*

    Development of Secondary Sex Characteristics   *109*

        BREAST CHANGES   *109*

        CHANGE OF VOICE   *109*

        PUBIC HAIR   *109*

        AXILLARY AND FACIAL HAIR   *110*

        SWEAT AND SEBACEOUS GLANDS   *110*

APPENDIX B   111

    Committees, Members, and Officers of the
    Group for the Advancement of Psychiatry

BIBLIOGRAPHY   117

INDEX   123

Normal Adolescence

Introduction

At this interval of rapid and extensive social change, it is timely and significant that a new publication should make available the developed knowledge and understanding of normal adolescence.

It is timely because nearly one-fifth of the nation's population is ten to twenty years of age. This growth interval is characterized by increases in youth activity, aggressiveness, mobility, and social interaction. At the same time, this nation and other industrially developed nations have not redesigned their social structures to provide for the significant participation of this next generation. Thus far, the public response has been to prolong the age of dependency by extending educational preparation for work. However, some starts have been made with work-study programs, volunteer service corps, and similar cooperative efforts among education, commerce, voluntary agencies, federal and local governments.

This book is significant because it is concerned with the normal adolescent in contrast to the extensive literature on the "delinquent adolescent," the "alienated adolescent," and other descriptive designations usually applied to this growth process and age status.

Today's youth is confronted not only with managing the changes accompanying psychobiological development, but with the unprecedented change of the impact of explosions in population, knowledge, technology, communications, and human aspirations. All adolescents are particularly vulnerable to the strains of this rapid social change. But selected populations of youth are subjected to additional hazards of less chance to reach their full potential due to circumstances of birth, family, and residence. These population groups include: (1) Negro, Puerto Rican, Mexican-American, and Indian youth, many of whom are from the lowest-income families; (2) some youth from urban slums and some of those in rural areas including the youth of migrant families; and (3) girls of low- and middle-income families who have been comparatively neglected in social planning which is accelerating for their male counterparts.

Normal Adolescence provides perspective and understanding of a generation that promises great hope for the future of man. This generation is seeking what is relevant to life and to know man's relation to man.

This book can be of value to professional staff of various disciplines working with youth: education, social work, medicine, law, recreation, the ministry, probation personnel, and others. It can also be useful to parents who seek to understand and to help eager young adolescents toward competent and satisfying adulthood.

This distinctive contribution of the Group for the Advancement of Psychiatry is in the best traditions of the nation.

It represents the hard work of a voluntary organization that has striven over the years to study and put to use accurate and correct understanding of the psychodynamics of our shifting social scene.

We are particularly grateful for this recent publication which concentrates the attention of the community on adolescents and on the interests of this critical segment of the population.

KATHERINE B. OETTINGER

Deputy Assistant Secretary for Family Planning and Population, U.S. Department of Health, Education, and Welfare

1

The Biology of Adolescence

Adolescence is a developmental phenomenon unique to man. The human infant is born in a relatively greater state of immaturity than are the young of other Primates. In the human being, hormonal and central nervous system maturation takes place over a period of years, not achieving culmination until puberty. In infrahuman animals, on the other hand, these maturations occur in a matter of weeks or months, with the concomitant early attainment of a relatively complete adaptive and procreative capacity. Similarly, the human being has only a few primitive adaptive reflex patterns at birth, whereas other animals are endowed with many more and considerably more complete inherited reflex patterns of adaptive behavior. Consequently, human offspring have a protracted period of dependency upon the mother or parents whereas the period of dependency of other animals, by comparison, is relatively short. Most importantly, in man significant patterns of behavior and adaptation are determined by individual experience and learning, much more than with other animals.

Man's nature as an interdependent social animal, with his unique adaptations of culture and society, has its basis in a specifically human pattern of biological maturation. The delay in attainment of full growth and sexual maturity in man would appear to be essential to his longer and richer development, and on this basis it has been suggested that adolescence is an important evolutionary trait.

Most of the specific content of our "human nature," whether evidenced in individual personality or group culture, is learned. This is true, for example, of the individual's response to the striking changes that occur from infancy to adulthood. Probably in no other mammal is there such a dramatic change in body proportions from the infant with his big brain and small helpless body to the full-sized adult. Masculinity and femininity, also, are not simply biological givens but must be learned. Other animals lack not only a human type of adolescence but a psychocultural latency period—a period of apparent quiescence or control of sexual drives occurring between early childhood and adolescence—in which individual development and learning make great strides, and the traditional group culture comes to bear through child training and educational practices. Thus, elements of human nature such as the incest taboo, semantic language, and ethical systems are acquired, not provided through heredity.

In this study we distinguish between *puberty,* which we regard as primarily a maturational, hormonal, and growth process, and *adolescence,* which in our view is a psychological, social, and maturational process initiated by puberty. This section of the report is a condensed statement of the pubertal, biological processes underlying adolescence.[1] An awareness of the anatomical and physiological changes confronting the growing individual is essential to the understanding of the resulting conflicts and the psychological and cultural solutions each individual forges in his struggle for mastery of his changed biological status.

The Complex Changes of Puberty

Puberty is characterized by the onset of hormonal activity which is under the influence of the central nervous system, especially the hypothalamus and the pituitary gland, both of which are located at the base of the brain. The major consequences are the increased elaboration of the adrenocortical and gonadal hormones and the production of mature ova and spermatozoa.

The age of onset, and possibly the nature, of the pubescent growth may have genetic familial determinants and may be affected additionally by culture, economy, and habitat. Clinical experience suggests that

[1] See Appendix A for additional information.

psychological events may influence the time sequence of pubertal changes. Physical growth and sexual maturation in both sexes may be retarded or hastened by emotional difficulties.

The age at which puberty is declared to begin depends in part upon the criteria of onset. In girls, breast budding and the beginning growth of pubic hair occur at an average age of 10 to 11 years, whereas menstruation occurs at about 11 to 13 years of age. In boys, the beginning of growth of pubic hair and of enlargement of the testicles occurs usually during the ages of 12 to 16 years, whereas enlargement of the penis and ejaculation take place from 13 to 17 years of age.

The increased elaboration of the gonadal and adrenocortical hormones leads to a broad spectrum of physiological and anatomical changes. These include: the development of primary and secondary sex characteristics; changes in size, weight, body proportions, and muscular development; related changes in strength, coordination, and skill. In some adolescents these changes occur very slowly and may extend for as long as five or six years. In others the changes may take place much more rapidly and be completed in one or two years. A rapid spurt of growth, though within the normal range, is particularly likely to produce troublesome psychological reactions, for the youngster finds it difficult to cope with so much change in a short period of time.

There are many interesting data about the pubertal growth spurt. The earlier it occurs in either sex, the more rapidly the associated changes take place. Adolescents who mature early are, on the average, heavier as adults than those who mature late. Boys who acquire a good deal of fat during adolescence are likely to have a broadening of the hips and fullness of the breasts which give them a somewhat feminine appearance. Certain changes tend to follow seasonal patterns. Weight tends to increase mostly in the fall, presumably because of fattening as opposed to the growth of other tissues. Increases in muscular strength and in height occur mostly in the spring. This pattern is evident already in early childhood but becomes exaggerated in adolescence.

Boys and girls from the age of one year through nine years grow at about the same rate. Male infants start life heavier by 1 per cent to 4 per cent, but the mean age at which maximum increase in height takes place is two years later in boys (14.8 years) than in girls (12.6 years); by ages 11 to 13, girls are taller and heavier than boys. At maturity, boys are 10 to 17 per cent heavier and 6 to 8 per cent taller than women. The male brain is about 11 per cent larger in volume than that of the female.

Physiologically, girls are older than boys from birth to maturity, and their earlier pubescence is only the culmination of their generally more precocious development. Differences in the rates of maturation of boys and girls are already present in the foetus, and are thought to begin with the primary gonadal differentiation at about the seventh week after conception.[2]

Differences in the nature of the growth changes in boys and girls derive from three factors. (1) In puberty, the differing sex hormones produce differential growth in the various body parts. Boys, for example, become broader in the shoulders and girls broader in the hips. (2) During the immediate prepubertal years, the lower extremities grow more rapidly than do the vertebrae. The more protracted growth in the male permits the development of longer legs relative to length of trunk. (3) Some body parts have a continuously higher rate of growth in one sex from the time of birth or even earlier. For example, males have a proportionately longer forearm in relation to the upper arm than do females. Such differentiation of course is not due to puberty.

Responses of Adolescents to Puberty

Following a long period of relatively slow growth, puberty produces marked changes in the organs involved in copulation and reproduction. For the male adolescent these changes are particularly important be-

---

[2] Maturation in the male is apparently slowed down by the presence of a Y-chromosome, as is suggested by the fact that the rate of skeletal maturation in Klinefelter's syndrome (a testicular dysfunction) where Y is present is distinctly slower than in Turner's syndrome (associated with ovarian agenesis and other congenital defects) where Y is absent.

cause his primary sex organs are external and readily seen, and because he commonly believes that the larger his penis and testicles, the greater his virility and potency. The male genitalia vary in size because of individual genetic differences, differences in androgen (male sex hormone) levels, and because individuals are at different points in the pubertal progression. Actually, size of genitalia has nothing to do with virility or potency. Nevertheless boys characteristically are concerned with the size of their genitalia, perhaps partly because of ignorance of this fact, and they anxiously make comparisons between themselves and other males.

In general, girls show less overt concern about their primary sex characteristics than do boys, mainly because their sexual organs are mostly within the body and not readily seen. Girls, however, are likely to develop a preoccupation of similar intensity with menstruation and the size of the breasts. The onset of menstruation in the girl signifies to her, her parents, and her peers (her contemporaries) that she has become sexually mature. The girl's concern with menstruation is heightened by the fact that the time of onset of menstruation varies greatly among girls, and also because the menstrual cycle commonly and normally is quite irregular for a year or two after the beginning of the menarche.

Secondary sex characteristics are distinguishing physical features of masculinity and femininity. In many ways, they are more important to teenagers than are the primary sex characteristics, in that they comprise the principal focus of sexual attraction between male and female. The male adolescent is much concerned about his height, the size of his muscles, the breadth of his shoulders, and the slimness of his hips. And the female carefully observes and often literally measures the development of her breasts and the broadening of her hips and worries about becoming too tall. Problems arise here, also, because characteristics such as fat and hair distribution, breast development, and voice changes vary greatly in their time of appearance and rate and extent of development. Not only do secondary sex characteristics show much variability among individuals of the same sex, but there also is the possibility that a member of one sex may develop, usually temporarily, one or more of the characteristics typical of the other sex. Yet, the relatively frequent appearance in one sex of physical attributes more typical of the other sex does not necessarily indicate hormonal malfunction. Bisexuality is a more or less normal aspect of development, at least in the sense that both the male androgenic and the female estrogenic hormones are present in both sexes. Body features can develop, fail to develop, or undergo change as a result of normal fluctuation in the balance between these hormones. An adolescent makes comparison between himself and his peers, and depending upon whether he feels his body arouses admiration or ridicule, his self-concept and self-esteem are either enhanced or impaired. The new awareness of body stimulates essentially new feelings and thoughts which require a remarkable shift in the integration of the adolescent.

Psychological and Social Aspects of Puberty

It seems appropriate here to take note of those psychological and social phenomena which stem quite directly from the anatomic and physiologic changes of puberty.

There is a most evident increase in preoccupation with the body. Shortness in boys and tallness in girls may cause genuine concern. Obesity commonly is a sensitive issue in adolescents of either sex. In girls, being overweight may make them feel unattractive. Depending upon the distribution of body fat, it may suggest either infantile qualities or a physical sexual precocity which has no counterpart in emotional development. In boys, obesity may cause embarrassment because it suggests a "babyish" quality or because excessive fat around the hips looks girlish.

Acne, an affliction unique to adolescence, is very common and almost universally causes emotional difficulties. Because acne is readily visible, it often serves as a focus for displaced guilt or concern about sexuality or "dirtiness," as though it somehow betrays one's secret thoughts and activities. A related phenomenon is the intense interest which some adolescents show in personal grooming, both to enhance their attractiveness and to conceal real or fancied deficiencies.

Adolescents tend to experience anxiety in unusually intense ways.

PSYCHOLOGICAL ASPECTS OF PUBERTY

They often are unduly conscious of the accompanying physical manifestations of sweating, muscular tension, increased heart rate, widened pulse pressure, and feelings of overwhelming fatigue. Sometimes the adolescent, being unaware of the causes for and signs of anxiety, regards these phenomena as evidence of illness. Adolescents sometimes develop a hypochondriacal preoccupation with their physical condition, to the detriment of their studies and social relationships.

Masturbation is a characteristic activity for most boys, but less so for girls, a smaller percentage of whom masturbate regularly. The changes in the genital organs contribute to a tendency toward increased masturbatory activity in both sexes. For some girls, early masturbation with an associated orgastic experience may result in abstinence from masturbation for several years. Accordingly, masturbatory conflicts are much more common and overt in male than in female adolescent development.

The basic instinctual forces are given considerable impetus by the physiologic changes of puberty. One manifestation of this is an increase in energy, which often overrides the thought processes and control mechanisms and discharges itself through action. Adolescents thus are prone to act impulsively in all sorts of ways, many of which will appear to be pathologic. A further determinant to the choice of the action mode may be the atmosphere of disapproval that surrounds the discharge of sexual tensions, more so in some subcultural groups than in others. Girls usually express their new-found maturity in styles of clothes and makeup which their parents are likely to consider "sexy" and inappropriate, whereas boys demand the car for dating and stay out too late. In girls the ultimate act of defiance is sexual behavior and promiscuity, whereas in boys it is more likely to be an aggressive act, such as stealing. Impulsive behavior in adolescence, particularly in the male, contributes to the fact that accidents constitute the major cause of death in the age group 15 to 19 years. The most frequent causes of death are automobile accidents, drownings, falls, and accidents with firearms.

Asceticism and intellectualization have been cited as prime defenses of the adolescent against the threat of increased sexual and aggressive urges. Asceticism is an attempt to deny entirely the instinctual drives.

Intellectualization similarly can be used in an attempt to cope with sexual and aggressive urges through thought processes, while also seeking to protect oneself from the shame and guilt associated with yielding to them.

Sooner or later, adolescents are confronted with the fact that their biological development has attained its ends. They are faced with the reality that their height, for example, now is permanent. The enthusiastic basketball player who at 16 is only five feet seven inches tall must cope with the knowledge that his goal of a career in that sport is far out of reach. Because it is and always will be crucially important to conform to peer standards, the sense of finality can be most distressing to some adolescents.

This discussion of the biology of adolescence conveys something of the complexity and stressful nature of the changes of puberty. The biological stimulus to the final movement from childhood into adulthood is common to all human beings. But, as shall be demonstrated, the nature of adolescence is determined not only by puberty but by the nature of a given adolescent's familial-cultural environment.

❧ 2

Cultural Factors in Adolescence

Proceeding now from consideration of the complexity of the biologic changes of puberty to the even greater variability in the cultural factors in adolescence, it is necessary to change and broaden the frame of reference. The term *society* denotes a continuing group of people who have developed certain relatively fixed ways of doing things which express their particular ways of viewing reality, and which employ specific symbols embodying these views. The society creates a whole universe of rules, laws, customs, mores, and practices to perpetuate the commonly accepted values and to cope with the various issues experienced by all members. All of these socially patterned ways of behaving constitute the society's *culture*.

The major physiologic changes that characterize the life cycle customarily become the subject of cultural preoccupation. Birth, death, marriage, childbirth, puberty, and senescence all provide focuses for special conduct, attitude, ritual, or some other standardized response. These are phases in the individual developmental cycle about which the group is likely to stipulate a group-defined position—a position that each member normally encounters and must cope with as a significant reality. Puberty, for example, inevitably calls attention to itself, and certain attitudes, values, and proscriptions, as well as ceremonies and rituals, impinge on each boy and girl experiencing this phase.

But it is not only the dramatic changes in growth and function that stimulate reactions in the society. The more gradual but no less meaningful social, psychological, and emotional maturation occurring in individual development during the transition into adulthood also is frequently accompanied by a wide variety of cultural definitions and reactions. The attainment of adulthood, for example, cannot be defined simply in terms of physical and physiologic changes, despite the obvious differences between the body and body functions of a child in early puberty and a fully grown adult. Girls and boys may develop quite precociously and attain full-fledged physical maturity as early as age 14, but this generally would not qualify them as adults.

Societies set their own criteria for adulthood, more often in terms of social tradition than biological maturity or even the psychological resolution of puberty. Biological, social, and psychological development and achievement may each proceed at a different pace, and the very differences may in themselves provide major stresses and stimuli to the growing youngster. Cultures vary markedly in their definitions of adulthood. Indeed, within a given culture there may be a whole series of degrees of adulthood that can be achieved by some of the members under certain conditions, yet can never be achieved by others under any conditions.

Criteria of Adulthood

In most, if not all, cultures there are two sets of criteria for defining or conceding adulthood; there are function definitions (e.g., earning one's own living) and status definitions (e.g., voting at age 21). Status criteria are easier to delineate, though they show wider divergence and in some instances rest upon highly capricious and arbitrary conventions. The formal accordance of adult status in any given society rests primarily upon the achievement of certain traditionally defined goals. In some societies, status adulthood may be accessible to only a few of the adults.

Functional adulthood rests upon different criteria and relates to the responsible roles the person assumes. This functional definition of adulthood is more tacit and implicit but exists nonetheless in terms of the assumption, or the delegation and assumption, of responsibilities. The four major categories of social responsibility which appear to exist in all societies are: self, mate, offspring, and society. Singly or in toto, these responsibilities must be assumed by some if not all members of the community. Yet it seems clear that one does not have to assume all of these responsibilities to be regarded as a functioning adult. In our culture, for example, note the bachelor, the unmarried schoolteacher, or the priest.

In order to appreciate the extreme variability of cultural definitions of adult function and adult status, it is necessary to clarify some terms. *Family of origin* refers to the family into which one was born. *Kinship family* refers to all the members related by blood. *Nuclear family* denotes the family consisting of the biological father, the biological mother, and their offspring. *Family of procreation* refers to the family of which one is a parent. *Uterine brotherhood* means born of the same mother.

Culture as "Environment" in Adolescence

In considering adolescence, one tends to have implicit preconceptions derived from his own adolescence in his own culture. But the categories of culture cannot be taken as absolute or inevitable. Cultural "environments" differ enormously and in startling ways, and they produce discernibly different standard adults. National temperament—for example, British reserve or French vivacity—is much more the result of different cultural expectancies and procedures toward children and adolescents than it is of racial heredity. Furthermore, because a society can apply pressure and produce stress in many areas of human development, different cultures can produce different character types and can even cause their own characteristic range and incidence of psychopathologic individuals or standardized deviants.

Basically, however, the cultural forms of each society must take their origin from the physiological differences between child and adult; they are shaped to deal with the contrasting biological tasks of childhood and of adulthood—being nurtured and providing nurture. But societies differ widely in their handling of both biological and status change. Physical maturity and status maturity are by no means the same. Self and society often appear to be antagonists, because society does require and attempt to enforce upon the individual varying kinds and degrees of suppression and control of the sexual and aggressive drives. Because of their different value systems, human societies seem almost to be unwitting experiments in the possibilities of "human nature," much as the nuclear family is the laboratory of individual personality.

To illustrate the wide divergence of adult functioning in a biological and psychological sense, and of adult-status "maturity," a striking example is given by the Mentawei of western Indonesia. Among the Mentawei a man may procreate a biological family, but only when his children are grown enough to support him can he formally adopt the children, marry their mother, and retire to the workless, semireligious status of father of a family. Here there is a spectacular lag of decades between functioning physiological maturity and a fully adult status accorded by society—far more of a lag, even, than in our own society. The system works well to gain Mentawei economic ends, for the man is motivated to produce and serve a family and to be faithful to one woman lest he lose the opportunity to finally get married and thus achieve full adult status.

Again, as far as the status of social fatherhood is concerned, biological fathers among the Nayar of Malabar never achieve this in a family of procreation; they remain lifelong unmarried *ciscisbei* (the male counterpart of concubines) of the mother. Instead, "fatherly" economic and social responsibilities come to a male by virtue of his uterine brotherhood to a mother from the same family of origin—i.e., to his sister. The biologic responsibilities of adult males and females to children are the same, since these are universal to the species, but they are redistributed from the family of procreation (which is our norm) to the family of origin. This economic and status displacement of the father by the maternal uncle, which is widespread in Oceania and elsewhere, derives from differing cultural emphases upon family of origin versus family of procreation. By way of contrast, our society nowadays minimizes the extended or kinship family but maximizes the marital family or family of procreation.

Sexual-functioning maturity and adult-status maturity are also widely disparate in the Polynesian cultures. Here social status and authority accrue to the first-born of first-born lineages, the eldest son of the senior lineage being the living embodiment of the ancestor god and repository of the *mana* of divine kingship, a status hedged about by taboos. Younger sons in successive lineages make up the pyramid of society, the youngest sons of the most junior lineages being at the bottom of the heap. Along with this social structure, many Polynesian societies have an institutionalized youth group, the *kahioi,* who provide feasts, entertainment, and sexual hospitality to tribal visitors. Sexual functioning is by no means prohibited to the youth group, but they must remain unmarried and childless to stay in it. Nor is membership in the youth group a function of chronological age. Thus there may be a younger son in a junior lineage who had tentatively married, later divorced his wife, killed his children, and rejoined the youth group—a *kahioi* 40 or 50 years old who never made the grade to social-status adulthood. The sop of irresponsible and promiscuous sexuality is thrown to the *kahioi,* of whatever age, but he never achieves the social status of founder of a lineage. Sexual-functioning maturity and social-status maturity thus are quite different from each other in societies with *kahioi.* Sexual potential is biologically given, but status must be socially achieved and accorded—as, indeed, in all societies. *Kahioi* may be remotely related culturally to the custom of the Nambutiri Brahmans of Malabar, among whom strict primogeniture (granting a special status to the first-born son) allows only the eldest son to marry, the younger sons becoming the statusless *ciscisbei* of Nayar women.

Throughout Oceania the emphasis, in general, is on status, not on sexual functioning, as the criterion of adulthood. In much of Oceania, pubescent boys can no longer sleep in their parents' house but must creep into the houses of eligible girls and sleep with them, and creep out again before dawn. Premarital "sleep-crawling" is also found among the Dobuans of Melanesia, where the line of descent is via the maternal side of the family. The boy continues this practice until he is "captured" in marriage by the girl's family, whereupon economic responsibilities are thrust upon him. In parts of Borneo even a husband must "sleep-crawl" to his wife, under pain of ridicule and embarrassment if caught. Here his sexual prerogative is officially discountenanced, but not his status as socio-economic husband; and here, as among the Mentawei, it is the man who is struggling for the status of marriage, not the woman, as in Western societies.

Nevertheless, universals do remain in the contrast of children and adults. Regardless of how the tasks of child-rearing are redistributed among various status and function categories, the tasks must still be carried out. Socio-economic responsibility for children, rather than sexual reproduction per se, would seem perhaps the ultimate criterion of adult status in most of the world.

Western Culture as Environment in Adolescence

In our culture, there exist a profusion and a confusion of different function definitions and status definitions of adulthood. In the category of status criteria, there is a whole range of different ages at which one becomes officially an adult in one manner but not necessarily in others. The first is the age of 12, after which one is an "adult" as regards theaters, movie houses, airlines, and so on. This first change of status confers no privileges whatsoever, only the penalty of having to pay more. The next general age post is 16. At this age, in most states, a person can obtain a driver's license; and he is released from many of the restrictions of the child labor laws. Both of these changes of status essentially do permit increased adult privileges. The young person does not have to work but may do so under certain conditions if he wishes. His legal right to drive is generally as unrestricted as that of his elders, but equivalent legal adult responsibility for his driving is seldom expected or enforced by the courts.

An even greater status change occurs at age 18. Males are then adults by decree of Congress for purposes of war and are subject to the draft. This is also the age after which, in many but not all states, young people may marry without parental consent. Often, however, they may legally toast their marriage only with beer—not with stronger alcoholic beverages. Thus we have the status paradox of the married soldier who may not enter a bar and drink, and who cannot vote, but who can procreate and kill. A girl at this age, again in most but not all states, may now consent to sexual intercourse, from the standpoint of law. If she were to have intercourse while younger than age 18, she would be considered to have been raped, regardless of the circumstances.

The final status change comes at age 21, when all the privileges and responsibilities of adulthood are legally invested in the young man or woman. The right to vote, the right to drink, eligibility for most public offices, the ability to enter into a binding financial contract, and full penalties for criminal transgressions—all are attendant upon reaching one's majority. Formal adult legal status should not be confused with the various levels of adult function or of respect status, which may continue to mount throughout life. The dean of a law school or the president of a mammoth corporation has no more legally conferred privileges and responsibilities because of age alone than does the 21-year-old undergraduate or café waitress.

In the category of function criteria, the definitions of adulthood in our culture are infinitely more complex and confused. Very few 12-year-old airline passengers who pay an adult's fare fulfill any adult role. Many 14-year-old girls are capable of bearing children and thus of functioning sexually as adults, yet there are no status categories to make this meaningful. Indeed, this functional capacity carries only potential penalty. The previously cited late-teenage soldier is a perfect example of an individual functioning as an adult in many roles without actually having full adult status. Conversely, the automatic investiture of full adult status at age 21 in no way guarantees that all such individuals will function as adults, emotionally or otherwise.

Earlier we defined functional adulthood as the assumption of one or more of the responsibilities for self, mate, offspring, and society. From this point of view, adult function after the mid-teens is quite unrelated to age, which is the basis of our definition of adult status. Many an 18-year-old is self-sufficient, yet many 23-year-olds are still in school and partly or totally dependent. These same 23-year-old graduate students may have wives and children and may admirably fulfill many family responsibilities even while unable to support themselves. In the more highly specialized professions, a man may not be fully self-sufficient—that is, as an economically functioning adult—

until his middle or late 30s, in spite of his having otherwise functioned as an adult quite well for as long as 15 years.

Adult function and adult status appear to find definition in a series of stages, and the two are integrated but little or not at all. The social definition of a functioning adult would seem to be achieved in Western civilization when he first assumes full responsibility for himself. This generally follows the attainment of a relatively stable mental and emotional equilibrium, a characteristic of the psychological offset of adolescence. Ordinarily, responsibilities are assumed for self, mate, offspring, and society in that order. For purposes of cross-cultural comparisons of adolescence and its psychological resolution, definitions of adult function would appear to be more basic and useful than formal definitions of adult status. The nature, quality, and timing of an individual's function are much more dependent upon his inner conflicts and his solutions of them than is his status, which may, as in our culture, be awarded or withheld despite function.

Universal Tasks of Adolescence

Are there any universals in the tasks of adolescence that transcend cultural differences and thus apply to all individuals? It has already been noted that man is a learning animal, and all adolescents therefore must learn, though what they learn differs from one culture to another. Also, the incest taboo is universal and, in general, relates to all parents and their children; in its basic form—the taboo on mother-son incest—there is no known exception. Thus, the adolescent has enforced upon him the invariable task of moving from his family of origin to a different (his own) family of procreation; to assume adult procreative function, he must sever close ties with the nuclear family and establish them with blood strangers. Another common denominator is the change from being nurtured to providing nurture. Finally, regardless of the surrounding culture, each adolescent normally is expected to learn how to work and how to love, both of these abilities being necessary to his functioning as an adult.

Biologically, the same needs and drives exist throughout the species;

culturally, alternative models are offered for their satisfaction; and psychologically, in the effort to reconcile his drives with cultural decrees, the adolescent in any culture employs previously developed, identical defense mechanisms such as repression, denial, and projection.

Cultural Facilitation and Inhibition at Adolescence

Each society has cultural commitments it regards as good. These commitments may not, in truth, be appropriate to the current world of reality, and certainly adolescents may not always regard them as immediately desirable. Nevertheless, the problem for society persists: how to fit new organisms into the older cultural context, how to make individuals achieve the kinds of discipline over their sexual and aggressive drives which are prescribed, preferred, or adaptive in a specific society and culture.

But it is just here that adult cultural judgment is so diverse and variable. Christian culture, for example, requires a relatively heavy repression and denial of direct aggressive drives. The individual is expected to cope with his aggressive drives only through a variety of defensive maneuvers. Among them are projection of his own inner self onto external forces such as "bad" teachers or officers of the law; self-disapproval for harboring sinful, destructive thoughts; sublimation into competitive endeavor such as dancing or sports; or identification with cultural heroes. By contrast, however, in some head-hunting and cannibalistic Indonesian and Melanesian groups, the direct expression of aggression is demanded and enforced to such a degree as to arouse anxieties in the individual which require containment through ritual, or expression in bizarre but (for the society) standardized, psychotic (insane) behavior. Similarly, the cultural demands for stylized aggression in Plains Indian warfare were often enough such an intolerable psychic burden for the individual as to create a standardized social deviant, the berdache: the "not-man," who may hunt, marry, and even procreate children but who wears women's clothes and who can never go on the warpath to take scalps—or to risk his

35

own. If the critical definition of a man in the Plains is a male person who goes on the warpath and takes scalps, then the berdache is a "not-man" and must be socially so signalized in his clothing, no matter what his activities as a male. Similarly, if head-taking is the criterion of ritual manhood or the requirement for marriage in the Wa States, Borneo, or New Guinea, then of course many males will attempt this cultural hurdle, at whatever individual psychic cost. Perhaps it is well that an adolescent now and again questions the goals proffered him by the adults in his society.

Cultures differ considerably in the way they facilitate or inhibit the attainment of full maturity. Many primitive societies appear to begrudge adult status and to demand that the individual prove his manhood in various ways from scalp-collecting or head-hunting to undergoing a painful and threatening puberty ordeal, with various bodily, significantly often genital, mutilations. And it may be that the least stressful and psychologically most secure way of achieving adult status is to be made a man, magically, by the puberty ordeal or initiation. If the skin, teeth, or genitals are altered in the process, one at least has, so to speak, a documented bodily proof of his adult status, and if the puberty ordeal contains threatening elements, they are at least circumscribed and delimited in time. A similar but more refined example from Jewish culture is the bar mitzvah ceremony.

Adolescence may be stressful, then, not solely for biological reasons but because of the pressures and demands that culture exerts upon the developing child. It has been suggested that in Samoa adolescence is relatively free of stress and turmoil because the Samoan culture allows its young people considerable freedom in their sexual behavior. Here, the physiological and the functional aspects of sexuality tend to coincide in the individual's life cycle, and his psychological problems are not focused around sexuality. If the function of eating, instead of sexual functioning, were the focus of massive cultural repressions and prohibitions, then eating might become a greater focus than sex for the development of emotional disturbance.

It is conceivable that cultural values for which there was a valid reason at one time—for example, sanctions for virginity associated with the custom of wife purchase, or the complete prohibition of pre-marital sexual relations at a time when conception and venereal diseases could not be controlled—may warrant re-evaluation when social, economic, and technological conditions have changed.

Again in Samoa, the gap between adult and child functions is minimized by the custom of having slightly elder siblings rather than adults provide the most immediate care for younger brothers and sisters. Consequently there is no great disparity in age and power between socializer and socialized, and this may help explain why Samoans have less anguish over power struggles than do Americans, in whose childhood the parents, comparatively, are omnipresent and seemingly omnipotent.

In much of Negro Africa, life membership in the same successively promoted "age group" achieves transition to adult status for the individual not only with the reassuring mutual example of peers but also with the powerful support of the adult culture. This system may suffer, however, for lack of individual freedom, spontaneity, variety, and adaptive social change. Initiation, a painful and threatening ordeal, may successfully achieve only the "authoritarian personality" of tribal orthodoxy and a compulsive, unreflecting loyalty to tradition.

For adolescents, *rites de passage* undoubtedly ease status transitions psychologically, and, in effect, such "rites" are provided in our culture. Qualifying for a driver's license at age 16 is essentially a *rite de passage,* certainly so in the mind of the adolescent. Again, the bar mitzvah is a socially useful and psychologically meaningful ritual in a tradition that emphasizes patriarchal leadership and responsibility. Similarly, in societies that emphasize the importance of virginity, a young woman may need a church wedding with all of its accouterments in order to dramatize psychologically her marked change of status. The male, somewhat less burdened with sexual repression, may well be content with a marriage before a civil magistrate. Perhaps job and fatherhood represent more critical areas for the young male adult than does sexuality, for it is in job and fatherhood that his important status tests lie. It is of interest to note that adolescents often invent their own *rites de passage,* such as "joining the crowd" in drinking to the point of nausea or stupefaction, or submitting to the primitive hazing practices associated with achieving membership in a college fraternity.

It is in relative terms, then, that one must consider adolescence in contemporary Judaeo-Christian culture and attempt to understand its manifestations and significance. This cannot be accomplished with any degree of completeness or finality. Not only is the magnitude of the task overwhelming, but the conditions of our culture and of our reality are constantly changing, and today's observations and conclusions soon belong to yesterday. Nevertheless, we may be able to sketch the matrix of our culture in relation to adolescence as it currently exists.

Adolescence in the American Middle Class

There are a number of reasons for choosing to focus discussion on the American middle-class culture and the adolescent of that culture: the middle class embraces the greatest proportion of our population; middle-class cultural attitudes are more widespread and affect more people than do those of any firmly delineated subcultural groups; and more reliable information is available about middle-class adolescence. Other class and regional, subcultural differences, of course, need to be taken into account. For example, southern Appalachian personality, bred in isolated, homogeneous rural culture, has a fundamentalist stolidity which, by comparison, makes urban middle-class excitability and restlessness appear as something antic; and, conversely, these Southern rural whites seem to be appallingly lacking in the motivations and goals of urban, middle-class culture. In urban Negro ghettos, individual "success," in middle-class terms, depends far more upon accidental emotional factors, relationship to authority, and opportunities for identification than upon a given family of origin. Siblings in the same family may therefore vary widely in their career trajectories.

Subcultural mores always somewhat overlap the main body of any culture, just as minority attitudes inject themselves into, and complicate, any generalizations about majority opinions. This discussion, therefore, will have some application outside of the middle-class majority. At the same time we are fully cognizant of the unavoidable oversimplification and overgeneralization attendant upon any brief discussion of so immense a phenomenon as the American middle class.

Certain qualities and distinguishing features help define and characterize adolescence in the American middle class. Of major importance are the facts that adolescence is a well-delineated stage of development and that adolescents form a special, self-conscious status group. This is by no means true in all cultures. Perhaps at no other time in history and in no other culture could one find so much attention being focused upon the adolescents. Products, advertising, entertainment, books, and newspaper columns are often designed for and aimed at this particular age group, and today they offer a special market and wield tremendous purchasing power. At one time a 15-year-old would have been referred to as a child or a youngster, but now he is known as a teenager—a term that denotes a large, influential, and important status group. The teenager has become very conscious of his special status. He is eager for the accompanying privileges, impatient or downright defiant of the restrictions, and not a little cocky about the vaguely defined power his group wields.

Closely related to the status of adolescents as a separate group is their intense and almost exclusive allegiance to the peer group. The adolescent peer group has its own forms and standards for fashions, fads, dancing, music, recreation, dating practices, vocabulary, etc., and all of this appears to be quite impervious to adult influence. This description is not limited only to the overtly rebellious adolescents. It portrays a frame of mind which is more or less characteristic of all adolescents, even those who are outwardly compliant.

The peer group is particularly important as a strong support to teenagers, both individually and collectively, in their characteristic questioning and challenging of adult values and cultural institutions. Younger children may protest and rebel, but their dependency and immaturity keep them much more closely tied to their parents than to their peers. Adolescents are able, then, to subject the cultural values learned in earlier childhood to a careful and sometimes devastating scrutiny and criticism to determine their applicability to the world of today, as it is seen by adolescents. Some adolescents appear not to accept any adult values, even superficially; some pass through a phase of experimentation with many different value systems, as a part of their search for identity; some feel the necessity of accepting adult values so as to survive in an adult-defined world; some achieve a close, positive identification with adults and their values but then fear loss of their newly developing independence and autonomy through absorption by the adult.

Another distinguishing feature of middle-class adolescence is what might be called its "hiatus status." Adolescents are no longer considered to be children, and yet they are not really expected to take their position in the adult world. They have some adult privileges (status) but are not expected to take on full adult responsibilities (functions). Though this hiatus status has many frustrating aspects, it also has some tempting gratifications. The transgressions of adolescents, even those which occur within such categories of adult status as driving, are often looked upon with tolerance. Adolescents are not usually required to assume full financial responsibility for themselves. Even though a boy may be earning enough money to meet his own expenses, most middle-class parents still expect to continue paying some of the bills. Of those adolescents who achieve the adult status of being married, thereby becoming legally emancipated, many still will receive a large degree of economic support from their parents, because the young husband or wife or both are in school. Adolescents may even succumb to the seductive and persuasive temptation to remain adolescent, enjoying a large measure of adult status and privilege while avoiding the responsibilities implied in acceptance of the adult role. Such over-aged, "professional" adolescents are a unique by-product of this particular aspect of our culture, and they contrast sharply with those ambitious adolescents who are impatient to enter the adult world and assume all of the adult responsibilities.

The hiatus status of adolescence with the granting of many adult privileges to those still technically adolescent leads to a paradoxically reversed situation. The acceleration of the granting of privileges to young people has the effect of telescoping the generations and obscuring adult-child differences. Examples may be seen in the earlier dating, increased buying power, and greater mobility of adolescents today. This quasi-adulthood does not make adults of adolescents, nor does it negate adolescent status. But it does strip adulthood of many of its traditionally distinguishing prerogatives.

Middle-class attitudes toward individuality versus conformity also may provide the basis for conflict. Traditionally, American society has stressed freedom of the individual, including choice of career. Self-fulfillment in an open society which provides "vertical mobility" means "finding oneself" in one of many fully accessible roles suitable to the special capacities of the individual. This frequently requires repudiation and leaving behind one's group of origin. Our history books inculcate in the child an admiration for the self-determined, often rebellious individuals who indeed greatly shaped our world through their very individuality. Today, however, our society also places a considerable emphasis on adaptive conformity, whether mediated unconsciously in training or even as an overtly stated goal: in order to "get ahead" one must "fit in" and not be too different. Adolescents are aware of the contradictory nature of these parental and cultural attitudes and tend to see them as an example of adult hypocrisy. They often feel that the pursuit of either one of these goals, individuality or conformity, incurs disapproval, and they find it difficult to embrace both at once. The implied freedom of choice necessary to the unique individuation which our culture so much desires appears to the adolescent to be countermanded by the emphasis on conformity. The result is frustration and conflict, or an avoidance of conflict by "choosing" to go in one direction or the other.

A primary determinant to middle-class adolescence is the fact that middle-class society is organized so exclusively around the nuclear family as opposed to the extended family. The biological mother and father and their offspring live together in a home which usually is not shared with others, and nearly all of the discipline and the culturally determined attitudes about child-rearing are conveyed to the child by his parents, at least during the preschool years. While our culture is still officially patrilineal (line of descent via the male side of the family), kinship ties tend nowadays to be important only legally. Paternal and maternal roles may be delegated (usually quite temporarily), but are not routinely distributed beyond the biological mother and father to other relatives. The increasing tendency for married couples to move away from their place of birth and to live separately from their elders and relatives further reduces the significance of relatives to the children. Elder siblings are required to carry little or no responsibility for the care of the younger children, and parents tend to regard the children as being equal to each other regardless of age. This family configuration means that children grow up in a society of competitive siblings or playmates, a kind of status group distinctly separate from the mother and father. And it also means that the children direct most of their conflict and aggression toward the biological parents rather than toward a multiplicity of parent surrogates. This early childhood period, in which culture and authority are mediated primarily by the parents, sets the stage for later childhood and adolescence. So, when other persons of authority come into a child's life, he perceives them more as extensions or copies of the parents than as new and different individuals, and cultural values and institutions also tend to be seen only as they were interpreted by the parents.

Another of the major cultural influences on adolescence is our "middle-class morality." This term includes morals in their usual sense, their derivatives in child-rearing techniques and attitudes, and, most particularly, the shifting of values so clearly observable in contemporary middle-class society. Some moral issues have intensified in significance, others have declined. Many attitudes that used to be bulwarks of society, such as the unquestioning belief in a traditional religion, have diminished as truly shaping forces.

The weakening of conviction and belief in the established value systems also contributes to the inconsistency between proclaimed attitudes and observable behavior. For better or worse the "official" standards always change more slowly than actual behavior. Whereas attitudes favoring greater sexual freedom can be discerned among some of the clergy as well as others who seriously appraise the morality of our culture, the long-established, prohibitive standards continue to be vigorously defended. The virtue of virginity, the ideal of sexual abstinence and "purity" until marriage, the concepts of carnal sin and "dirty" sex still are a part of the proclaimed ethic in a large proportion of our society. The same is true of the strong taboo against the direct expression of aggression, although aggression does not carry the same degree of reproach as does sexuality.

Middle-class culture, of course, is not monolithic in sexual attitudes. There are sizable segments of the population, particularly the more sophisticated adults in the larger urban areas, that openly disagree with the prohibitive morality of their parents and grandparents and that try to rear their children accordingly. But most observers would regard these elements as exponents of change rather than as arbiters of current majority attitudes. Middle-class culture, for the most part, does not provide for a guilt-free orgastic sexual outlet between puberty and marriage.

One result of this kind of morality is that the adolescent has both the tremendous task of controlling his sexual feelings and urges, and the heavy burden of guilt arising from the almost inevitable failure to do so. Referring again to the emphasis middle-class culture places on the nuclear family, it seems likely that this plays an important role in intensifying the adolescent sexual conflict by focusing virtually all of the developing child's sexual feelings on his biological parents.

Adolescents find it very difficult to live by the culturally prescribed sexual morality, and they often pay a high price emotionally in attempting to do so. Many have just about given up making the effort, for no one whose childhood was lived in the context of a prohibitive morality can be really free of its legacy of sexual guilt. The nature of the dilemma determines the standard variations of adolescent efforts at solution of the problem: rebellion against sexual ethics and denial of conscience; early dependent marriage; early marriage with withdrawal from the socio-economic struggle; repudiation of sexual prohibitions in good faith and sincerity but with unavoidable unconscious guilt; subordination of sex to, and contamination of sex with, competitive goals; or strong repression of sexuality, with the likelihood of subsequent mental or emotional disorder. The attitudes of middle-class culture make it very nearly impossible for adolescents to employ, in a healthy way, the alternatives to such modes of behavior, namely, masturbation or sexual intimacies with the opposite sex, appropriate to the individual's age and degree of emotional maturity.

This generalized view of middle-class morality as being prohibitive and inhibitive may seem to be contradicted by the obvious current emphasis upon sex in our culture. Note the content of much of what is expressed through the media of mass communication and the child-rearing practices of many parents who condone and sometimes foster such things as dating and the wearing of make-up and sexually provocative clothing at a very early age. These attitudes usually are more sexually stimulating than truly permissive, however, and they tend only to add to the sexual conflict. In most families, particularly in some subcultural groups, the line is firmly drawn at sexual intercourse, or even at masturbation. The degree of sexual behavior which is permitted also differs for boys as against girls. For the girl it is competitive "sexiness," not functional sexuality, that is fostered. The attitude of many adults is paraphrased in the expression, "Hang your clothes on a hickory limb but don't go near the water."

Discontinuity of Role from Childhood to Adulthood

While there are obvious biological and functional differences between child and adult, cultures may polarize these distinctions to the detriment of individual growth. This can happen if the child and adult roles are defined in such a rigid and sharply contrasting way that one role does not lead naturally and logically into the other. Similarly, contradictory training may interfere with normal role maturation. As adulthood approaches, difficulties in adjustment are likely to confront the adolescent who has been too stringently inculcated with attitudes of dependency, obedience, and abstinence from sexual behavior; particularly so when the criteria of success in adulthood are independence, self-direction, assumption of responsibility, and sexual performance. Thus an adolescent who has adapted too well in his role as a child and has become too comfortable with it finds it difficult to assume his new role as an adult.

It is possible, then, that our social forms are not as well-suited for training children to become adults as for training them to be successful children. For the adolescent, these contrastively defined roles tend to place him in the position of being damned if he tries to act like an adult and damned if he doesn't. As a result, adolescents become "problems" to adults as well as to themselves.

The Papago Indians, among others, achieve a more successful continuity of role training; even the small child is rewarded for economic and other behavior befitting the future adult, and thus he begins in childhood to be trained for successful adulthood. This does not mean that the adult must abdicate the responsibilities of adulthood, or cease to be a model for the child, or pretend to a spurious and seductive siblinghood with the child (as in wanting to be regarded as a pal rather than a parent). It does mean that whatever training is imposed upon a child will be carried by him into adulthood, and that he and his society will suffer if the training ill fits the child for the adult world.

These brief comments indicate in part the degree of interaction of definitive cultural attitudes and adolescence. A further dimension is added when some cultural institutions have in fact begun to lose meaning and force for the adults who continue to uphold them. The adolescent is a particularly sharp observer of adult culture, and even the most casual observation reveals a decreasing adherence to the Judaeo-Christian ethic, which is still the "official" ethic of our culture. The adolescent perceives that such things as financial success, respectability, and the holding of public office often seem to bear little relationship to the individual's ethical behavior, and that failure to live by traditional values is not necessarily followed by unpleasant consequences.

It has been suggested that it is not frustration alone that makes children neurotic, but also the lack of ultimate cultural rewards for the frustration the child must endure. Clearly, middle-class adolescents are often caught in this trap. There was once a time (though this could sound like a fairy tale to today's young people) when a person could plan his future on the basis of commitments made during and at the end of adolescence. Certain things in the community happened to those who accepted and at least tried to live by the cultural values. If these things were important to the young person, he knew how to get them. The approved modes of harnessing one's instinctual drives had practical and demonstrable meaning. Quite other life paths lay open to those who repudiated middle-class morality, and quite other consequences, too, which were edifyingly visible and sure. The two types of life commitment were mutually exclusive.

This description perhaps is overgeneralized but, nonetheless, there is an important difference between an adult society that as a whole believes in and tries to live by its own moral values and one that does not. There is often little consonance between the expressed middle-class values and actual adult behavior. Caught in their own confusion, adults may be at a loss to demonstrate to adolescents any consistent rewards in their own lives which derive from accepting the "official" ethic. The adult world therefore often appears to adolescent eyes to operate upon principles contrary to honesty and other espoused cultural values.

Ours is a competitive technological society, and this fact also shapes the adolescent stage of development. The adult world places emphasis upon winning the struggle for status and position, and since the outcome rather than the means is emphasized, ability is often subordinated to agility. A society in which vertical social mobility is not only possible but applauded, automatically makes such advancement a high-priority goal. Children very early are initiated into this mêlée through the competitive sibling structure of our nuclear family unit, and are kept aware of this orientation throughout their school and playground activities. Grading systems also maintain this emphasis, and thoughtful teachers of adolescents complain that the real goal of many of their pupils is "second-guessing" the teacher and getting the grades, rather than learning for the sake of its lasting benefits.

Increasing technology, with its demand for more and more education, before one is eligible to compete, meanwhile adds to the real tasks of adolescence. There are fewer and fewer jobs for the unskilled and semiskilled, and those young people who cannot or do not accept the challenge of gaining an adequate education generally are doomed to a substandard socio-economic existence. On the other hand, the demand for more and more education and the resulting longer period of dependency exist alongside the relatively unchanging prohibitions against adolescent sexuality. Thus the gap between physical sexual maturity and the socio-economic readiness for self-sufficiency and marriage becomes still wider.

Some adolescent problems that are insignificant or invisible in more primitive societies loom quite large, and understandably so, in our society. One of these is the problem of identity. In simpler societies that offer only two sex-defined role models there is little problem. The quest for identity is a problem, however, in the more complex cultures which are characterized by rapid social change, so that the father may become outmoded as a model for his son; by geographic mobility, so that cultural models are constantly changing; by emphasis on individuality with great freedom of choice; by a high degree of complexity, in which there are many models from which to choose; and by "classlessness," wherein everyone strives to upgrade his social status. The fact that these conditions pose problems for the adolescent in his quest for identity is counterbalanced, however, by the fact that they also offer a richness of choice which our culture certainly would not wish to forego.

All of these factors complicating the adolescents' search for identity exist in our middle-class culture, and simultaneously increase both the rewards and the burdens of the task. Such a multiplicity of possible future selves has probably seldom before been available to eager, healthy youngsters. The adolescent clearly knows of these relatively limitless choices that have been constantly in evidence throughout his childhood years. But identity by no means automatically accrues to the individual as he grows older. Thus there arises not only the time-consuming necessity to experiment and choose, but also the possibility for neurotic conflict and inappropriate choice.

A further complication to the task of establishing identity lies in the increasing diffusion of male and female parental roles and the blurring of the traditional lines of distinction between the sexes. The mother and father both may be working, and in many cases the mother handles the finances. "Togetherness" means that the father shares in the housework and baby care after he comes home from work. There also has been a great increase in the role possibilities for females so that, today, few fields remain closed to women. There are, for example, many female policewomen and business executives —counterparts, so to speak, of the male hairdressers and dress designers. In such a society, sex-defined roles become ambiguous, and the developing child may receive few clear clues, other than anatomical, to sex differentiation. Since the fact remains that "anatomy is destiny," at least as regards the male and female roles in procreation, the adolescent is left to struggle with his most momentous identity task, sexual identity, in the absence of clearly sex-defined roles. Thus the richly varied, changing, and individually fulfilling legacy of un-limited identity alternatives is a bequest with strings attached, and one sees many adolescents who have become tangled in the strings as well as many who have benefited from the gift.

Rapid Social Change as a Problem of Adolescence

Our times have been called the Age of Anxiety, and certainly the quality of mounting uncertainty has immeasurable consequences for the adolescent. It is difficult to be certain, however, that this attribute is peculiar to our culture and time. Surely the future has never been truly certain for any society at any time, and there have been other historical instances of cultural despair. But if one may take evidence from the recorded attitudes of earlier periods in our own culture, there usually has been a prevailing, generally accepted fantasy that the future was predictable and secure. Even if dangers lay ahead, specific measures formulated by the mentors of society would surely avert them.

Today there is no such preponderance of widely accepted prophets of security. Instead, much of current literature conveys prophecies of doom, retrospective analyses of what has gone wrong with humanity, exposés of the neurotic substructure of contemporary values and behavior, and a philosophy of "live for today for tomorrow you may be vaporized." Existential philosophy emphasizes that the only reality is the present moment of existence. Scientists engage repeatedly in public debates about whether mankind will or will not survive the next war, or the next bomb tests, or the next fifty years of population growth. The general attitude is that no one really knows what to do to keep *homo sapiens* from joining the dinosaurs, and anyone who believes that there is a solution to this problem is likely to be regarded with condescending skepticism.

Whether or not it is unique to our time and culture, the fact remains that adolescents are hardly ever given, and would find it hard to accept, the reassuring myth of a predictable future. When most adults have belief in the future, it provides a basis for youth to believe similarly, and to seek culturally continuous identities similar to those of the adults. When adults confess that they are lost, confused, and lack direction, it is not surprising that adolescents, driven as they are by the thrust of puberty, often repudiate adult values and at times give way to "orgies" of seemingly meaningless and sometimes destructive behavior. We should note, too, that adolescent culture itself changes with breathtaking rapidity. To today's college student, the "Joe College" of a few years ago is terribly outdated, and to a Peace Corps generation the stylized, social dropout, the beatnik, is rapidly becoming passé. Thus, whatever the identity the adolescent is striving to achieve, he may find the rug pulled out from under him by a succeeding adolescent generation.

It should now be clear that some of the manifestations of adolescence are not only specific to, but are partially caused by, the culture. Comparative anthropological considerations are useful to give perspective, to alert us to the arbitrariness and contingency of much of our cultural handling of adolescence, and even to offer possible alternatives and modifications. The biology of puberty is universal, but human reactions to puberty always occur within a particular culture, and adolescence becomes fully intelligible only through an awareness and understanding of the culture which surrounds it.

❧ 3

The Psychology of Adolescence

In adolescence, as in all other life stages, behavior is the result of the interaction taking place between the individual and his environment. The preceding chapters considered the biological aspect of individual development and the general cultural aspect of environment. In this chapter, the discussion will be focused on the dynamics of the internal psychological (intrapsychic)[1] functioning of the adolescent and his closer relationships with people (object relationships). As was indicated previously, the people of greatest importance to him are his parents and his peers. As he moves toward adulthood, however, he becomes increasingly subject to direct and indirect influence by others, even people in strikingly different and geographically distant cultures —note, today, the possibility of his serving in the Peace Corps or, ironically, the armed forces fighting the war in Vietnam.

The primary elements entering into the intrapsychic dynamics are: the forces and demands of the instinctual, sexual, and aggressive drives (the id); the mediating, executive part of personality which utilizes the uniquely human intellectual, language, and other capabilities in the task of maintaining psychological equilibrium while coping with demands from within the self and from the external world (the ego); the individual's own value system or conscience which embodies concepts of right and wrong, the moral imperatives, and his ideals (the superego). It is the adolescent's earlier, childhood development which

[1] The parentheses in this and the next paragraph indicate terms from psychoanalytic psychology which are used in this report.

has provided him with his personality structure, with certain characteristic ways of managing himself and of relating to others (adaptive and defensive techniques), and also with certain underlying conflicts.

The relative ease or difficulty with which the adolescent progresses through this stage of development is determined in large measure by his past experience and by the nature of the underlying intrapsychic conflicts, which now will be revived. Before proceeding to the discussion of adolescence per se, it is necessary to review those aspects of earlier development which are particularly relevant to the understanding of adolescence.

The Role of Childhood Experience

In infancy and early childhood the closest relationship for children of both sexes is with the mother. The mother normally provides not only the early nurturing experiences but also the weaning, toilet training, and the first disciplinary experiences. It is inevitable, therefore, that the child will be frustrated by the mother and develop mixed feelings toward her. These mixed feelings of love and resentment play an important role throughout childhood development, since they mean that the child can never feel entirely safe or secure in any relationship. They also support his tendency to use his developing capacity for imagination or fantasy to distort the meaning of certain of his observations and experiences, usually in such a way as to give them dangerous or frightening implications.

At about two or three years of age children try to find an answer for their curiosity about why some people have a penis and some do not. Whereas the child at this age or earlier can observe and take note of such an obvious anatomical sexual difference, he usually does not know about and could not readily comprehend the full facts of sexual differences (e.g., the internal sexual organs of the female). Accordingly, both boys and girls, even though told otherwise, tend to fantasy that the female is lacking a penis for reasons having to do with injury, punishment, or not being sufficiently loved by the mother. It is out of these fantasies and circumstances that children of both sexes develop what psychoanalysts term castration anxiety or a castration complex.

The problem of castration anxiety is resolved differently in the two sexes. In the girl, the initial reaction may be to deny to herself the fact that she has no penis, this for quite variable periods of time. She imagines, for example, that it is hidden away inside the body, or that it will grow out later. On the other hand, those girls who fairly readily accept that they have no penis usually become preoccupied for a time with the presumed reasons for their apparent anatomical lack, again through reality-distorting fantasies. They also may develop envy of the male, but this also is variable in degree and duration.

Because the girl previously had felt that the mother was frustrating her feelings of autonomy and omnipotence, she now tends to blame her mother for not having a penis. An important consequence is that, out of resentment toward the mother, she then turns to her father as the new primary object of her love. This initiates her oedipal phase which is characterized by strong feelings, both affectionate and sexual or erotic, toward her father with ambivalent and rivalrous feelings toward her mother.

In the boy, the presence of the valued penis poses the possibility that this organ may be lost, and castration anxiety thus is kept alive. Boys defend against this possibility in various ways. For example, some boys become fearful of any kind of body injury and behave passively, avoiding physical activity and roughhouse games; others unconsciously deny their fears and plunge headlong into activities which tend to be daring or risky, such as climbing trees, jumping from high places, or constructing underground "forts."

In the case of the boy, his early affectionate and dependent love relationship with his mother becomes complicated, at about four or five years of age, by his developing sexual feelings. Thus he enters his oedipal phase which is analogous to that of the girl, but with sexual feelings directed toward his mother and rivalrous feelings toward his father.

Under the most favorable circumstances the child gives up the close erotized relationship to the parent of the opposite sex and replaces it with a desexualized attitude of tenderness and affection. Simultaneously all incestuous urges or wishes are firmly repressed. And the rivalrous and often intensely ambivalent feelings toward the parent of the same sex are replaced by identification with that parent. This is a crucial step in the attainment of an appropriate and clearly defined sexual identity. The impetus for these changes is provided by the taboo against incest, the fear of punishment (castration) for the forbidden sexual urges, and the inevitable frustration of the child's sexual wishes toward the parent.

When the girl gives up her wishes toward her father, she may for a time be torn between identifying with her mother or regressing into infantile, dependent, and hostile interactions with her. It is necessary for the girl to maintain a rather rigid inhibition of her infantile needs in order to safeguard the new and more mature relationship. Frequently, resentment toward the mother lingers on and the oedipal conflict is not brought to a decisive solution. Fantasies involving love triangles, indicating that the girl unconsciously still rivals with mother for father, often persist in girls during adolescence. Sometimes the oedipal dilemma is not fully resolved until a girl marries and has her first child.

When the boy gives up his wishes toward his mother, he is not confronted by the threats of regression and return to dependency which exist in the girl's renewed relationship with her mother. The establishment of a stronger relationship with his father reinforces his strivings for independence. On the other hand, he does have misgivings about the loss of his infantile, dependent relationship with his mother. Although he cannot regain his former closeness with his mother, the boy can persist, much longer than the girl, in preoccupations and behavior characteristic of earlier stages of development. This is because the remnants of sexuality from infancy and early childhood are not associated with closeness to the father and therefore do not need to be so inhibited. The boy's resolution of the oedipal conflict normally is more decisive than that of the girl.

With the resolution of the oedipal conflict and the establishment of a reasonably firm identification with the parent of the same sex, the child enters the latency stage of development. This stage is characterized by a fairly stable equilibrium within the personality, maintained through an alliance between the ego and superego which together are able to control and modulate the instinctual drives. At one time it was thought that the actual strength of the drives was decreased in latency in comparison with the preceding developmental stages. It now is conceived that the strength of the instinctual drives remains essentially the same, but that a stronger ego curbs the sexual urges so that they are turned aside from direct expression. At the same time the aggressive drive can be fairly readily expressed, for example, in the socially approved and encouraged competitions of the elementary school years. Furthermore, some of the energy from the sexual drive is probably deflected into and absorbed by the aggressive impulses.

The latency stage of development is characteristic of our culture, in some ways uniquely. There are cultures in which sexual preoccupation and behavior are quite openly expressed by children throughout this age period, not appreciably different than in earlier years or in puberty. But in Western culture, the pattern described above does seem to be the norm. The latency stage provides a respite between the preceding stage of development and adolescence, during which the growth of the ego goes on at a great pace as it consolidates old functions and acquires new ones for coping with the drives and for adapting socially and intellectually.

As has been stated, the latency-age girl in her identification with her mother is relatively free of regressive sexual interests. She therefore moves, more quickly than the boy, in the direction of heterosexuality. She turns to the reality of the external world, manifesting great curiosity about sex, although at first not necessarily about the opposite sex. Whereas in earlier childhood her interest was in anatomical sex differences, she now is interested in sexual functions, e.g., menstruation, conception, and how the baby grows inside the body.

As the boy enters the latency stage, he at first repudiates girls, in part because he wishes to avoid being reminded of their penisless state, which to him is a proof that castration could happen. He commonly defends against this fear by turning toward other boys. He is reassured by the company of others of his own sex, and he forms "gangs" or clubs which characteristically exclude girls. The move of the boy toward heterosexuality therefore is delayed, and this is one of the factors accounting for the greater social and emotional maturity of the girl during the early school years.

To explore all of the precursors of the adolescent response would require an extensive review of childhood development. However, this selective discussion of the role of childhood experience should convey that adolescence, though a specific stage in its own right, is part of a continuum of development and is greatly influenced by what has gone before.

Preadolescence

The progressing changes in endocrine balance which have been going on since the age of 8 or 9 result in vague body sensations and emotional stirrings that are unsettling and premonitory of the pubertal changes still to come. In addition, in prepuberty there is a characteristic increase in activity and probably of energy, most likely on the same hormonal, biophysiological basis. The increase in energy at this time, however, does not appear to be associated with any significant change in the strength of the sexual drive, as will be the case in puberty. Children now play with increasing vigor but show little change in their behavior toward the opposite sex. An important factor in preadolescent psychology is the child's anticipation of puberty, which is stimulated in part by the effects of prepuberty and in part by a quite conscious awareness of what lies ahead. The development and behavior of adolescents are closely observed by preadolescents, as are the correlated attitudes of the parents and the culture.

As was stated previously, attitudes toward sexuality in our Western culture have been at best ambivalent. On the one hand sexual pleasure has been strongly condemned, and on the other hand there is a considerable exposure of children to sexuality through newspapers, magazines, books, movies, and television. Accordingly, parents tend to view the approach of their child's puberty with ambivalence, and this affects the way in which they prepare him for puberty. Usually, menstruation is discussed with girls, and masturbation (but less often ejaculation and nocturnal emission) with boys. Most children have asked some questions and been given some information about the anatomy and the functioning of the opposite sex, and about conception. But the subject of sexual intercourse and the matter of sexual feelings and sexual pleasure are usually avoided.

There is the added problem that even those parents who try to give helpful factual information to their children are likely to also communicate their ambivalence and fear of the dangers of sexual activity, because of their own anxiety and discomfort. There are other parents who avoid these issues entirely by simply remaining silent. Many school systems provide prepubertal children with some education in sexual matters, but as a rule this effort is not coordinated with parental efforts in the home. In many instances the educational effort fails to be of significant help to the child because the parent or educator does not take into account the child's need to discuss and correct the often distorted information and ideas he has acquired from other children and through his own imaginings.

As the preceding discussion would suggest, the preadolescent child is quite conflicted about sex. He receives information about it with mixed feelings of eagerness and apprehension, in part because of his own distorted fantasies. Frequently, newly provided sexual information seems to be promptly forgotten. A girl will insist to her mother, for example, that she was never told about menstruation, even though the last discussion of it took place only a month previously. If the school shows a film on reproduction, a child often will be unable to assimilate the information well enough to remember the main topics presented when asked about it later that evening. At times this rather amazing phenomenon may be due to a feigned ignorance in the service of secrecy, out of uneasiness with the subject matter or compliance with the cultural double standard. Frequently, though, it represents a genuine, unconscious denial of anxiety-producing knowledge.

The progression toward puberty normally proceeds rapidly. However, it usually takes place in secrecy in the private sexual explorations of the individual child and in the activities and discussions of preadolescent peer groups. Intensely curious and eager for sexual knowledge, children at this age search for it in novels, "romance" magazines, "nudie" magazines, and medical books, secret conversations with their peers, examination of their own bodies, and bedtime activities. In the peer groups, there usually is a somewhat older sibling or friend who has already and very noticeably entered puberty and whose body and actions are carefully observed and discussed. Within the privacy of these groups the sexual urges may not be greatly repressed. Group masturbatory play is fairly common among boys, with great interest being shown in the size of the penis and its sensations. In either boy or girl peer groups there is speculation about what the sexual experiences of adolescence and adulthood will be like. Such speculations and shared fantasies are built in part upon reality but frequently have an overlay of all the distortions, rumors, and wild tales that filter down to the youngsters from adults, older teenagers, books, jokes, and the like. These thoughts characteristically are expressed with a mixture of eager delight and giggling apprehension. Sometimes the groups may include both sexes and mutual exposure and exploration of genitals, but more typically the sexes are separate.

As in the latency stage, the preadolescent boy also is likely to be uneasy in close relationships with girls. He, too, tends to seek the reassuring company of other males. On the other hand, avoidance is not his only reaction toward girls. He begins to respond with interest to the girl's already evident interest in him, but his sexual feelings usually are masked by teasing and aggressive behavior. Also, boys at this age may evidence envy of the child-bearing capacity of the female. The counterpart of the tomboy girl who envies the male is the boy who collects and raises animals such as mice and tropical fish, a major share of his interest being in sexual reproduction, the observation of birth, and the garnering of offspring.

The preadolescent girl typically is aggressive and not very feminine in her pursuit of attention from boys. There usually is a resurgence of the earlier envy of the male which may be reflected in masculine, aggressive behavior amounting to a denial of femininity. Some girls find a temporary compromise solution in the role of the tomboy or the horseback-riding enthusiast, and others move more quickly toward femininity in roles such as the "junior miss" or the aspiring ballet dancer.

At this stage, one of the characteristic changes in both sexes is an increase in physical activity. In part, this is due to an increase in energy, but it is also an expression of the anxiety associated with approaching puberty and the revival of conflicts from earlier stages of development. There is a strong need for an outlet for the relief of tension. Usually there is an increase in appetite, sometimes amounting to voracity, which probably has both physiologic and psychologic roots. Hormonal changes initiate the very beginnings of the increase in growth which must be supported nutritionally; besides, eating is a way of easing anxiety and tension. The struggle between a desire for dependence upon mother and the wish for independence may also be revived. This can account for a regression in behavior characterized by disorderliness and dirtiness, provocative displays of "bathroom" humor, and a welling up of negativism, stubbornness, unruliness, and disobedience.

Some children attempt to ignore and deny the prepubertal stirrings, trying to control them with suppressive and repressive techniques. Such youngsters cling to the adaptive techniques of latency as if to postpone the imminent changes. Other youngsters react with regressive behavior. For example, a minor injury may evoke tears and whining in a boy who for a long time has ignored such an event; he suddenly behaves as if he were a very little boy. Similarly, some prepubertal girls insist on wearing little-girl clothes. Generally, repression is a less pathological defense than denial, since it is an overt and more readily reversible response to the beginning biological changes. Still other children look forward to puberty and welcome it. They seem disposed to grow up quickly, often too quickly in adult eyes. At times, though, such an eager embracing of puberty may be pathologic, serving mainly to solve a conflict with the parents by getting away from them. Such a precocious "maturity" is really a flight into a pseudo-adolescence and a pseudo-heterosexuality. But regardless of whether it is feared or welcomed, puberty does arrive, and its thrust imperatively propels the child into further psychological development.

The Beginning and Ending of Adolescence

THE ONSET

Adolescence begins with puberty. As the changes at puberty occur, there are corresponding changes in personality, not all of them necessarily displayed in overt behavior. There is considerable variation in the manner in which individuals cope with the events of puberty. For example, girls may deal with menstruation in very different ways. A girl may attempt to deny to herself that it has happened, and as a result she will evidence no anxiety or other overt reaction to the menstrual flow. Another girl may deal with it in the same basic way but reveal an increase in tomboyish behavior; she denies that menstruation has happened and behaves as though she were not becoming a woman. And still another girl may welcome menstruation as a clear sign of sexual maturity.

Even though a girl has denied her menarche as well as other signs of puberty, and her overt behavior has remained unchanged, she nevertheless will have entered adolescence. On the other hand, when the onset of puberty is delayed into the middle or late teens, the understandable concern with the delay in physical development is not an adolescent problem, according to our definition of the onset of adolescence.

THE PHASES

Adolescence can be divided into two major phases. The first phase is initiated by an increase in the strength of the instinctual forces. The child suddenly experiences strong erotic and aggressive impulses that seem to come from nowhere and clamor for expression. A boy who has been indifferent to observing his sister's undergarments lying about the house now begins to have sexual fantasies and feelings which result in pleasure, guilt, shame, and confusion. And he furthermore feels that he dare not tell anyone about this. His emotional equilibrium is upset, as evidenced by the repeated breakthrough of these impulses (for example, peeking on his sister in her bedroom or reaching out

59

to touch her body), or by the harshness and extremity of the means employed to control them (for example, intense waves of guilt and self-condemnation). In his conflictual struggle a boy might pick a fight with his sister, go to church and confess, masturbate, or suffer in silent anguish—or do all of these things. The ego is continually threatened and often is temporarily overwhelmed. In its attempt to re-establish equilibrium and maintain control it must expend excessive energy, sometimes paying the price of rigidity, loss of spontaneity, and inhibition of intellectual abilities. These latter factors may account for "the seventh- or eighth-grade slump" described by educators.

The first phase of adolescence usually ends in the middle teens and is followed by a second phase in which the balance of power between the ego and id shifts in favor of the ego. The factors causing this shift are by no means clear, but several possible explanations can be offered. (1) There may be an improved regularization and stabilization of the underlying hormonal and biological processes. (2) The fear and panic that accompany the beginning of puberty may diminish considerably as the still developing ego gains mastery over the new impulses, feels less threatened, and begins to function more effectively. An example of this would be the shift from the tantrums and outbursts of the early teens to the later attempts to use logic and rational argument to achieve one's goals. (3) A major shift in love interest normally takes place. Dating has begun, and the youngster gives up the former closeness to the parents, directing both dependency needs and sexual feelings toward the boy friend or girl friend. This shift, even though at first still colored by unconscious incestuous motives, nevertheless diminishes intrapsychic conflict and is a most important step toward the eventual choice of a marital partner. (4) The ego begins to utilize its increased capacity for the highest forms of abstract thinking, newly provided at this time apparently by the further biologic maturation. As part of his coping behavior, the teenager can begin to reason and argue, for example, about the validity of God and religion or the advantages of celibacy or of free love in an ideal society. Thus he can start to deal with the instinctual drives in fantasy and thought rather than by either impulsive action or excessive inhibition.

The observation that the adolescent in his middle or late teens begins to concern himself in a very personal and often intense way with such philosophic questions as the meaning of life and death, with religion, and with political and social issues, also lends support to the division of adolescence into two phases. At the same time this observation correlates with the fact that the adolescent at this age generally is much more amenable to reason and discussion and to psychotherapy or psychoanalysis than is the younger adolescent. The older adolescent is not nearly so frightened of his sexual and aggressive drives, and may be quite willing or even eager to join the analyst in the task of helping himself. The ego has gained a different orientation toward the id forces, and the adolescent can begin to use his faculties of self-observation and self-evaluation and his intellectual abilities in seeking to understand himself. Although there is greater psychological stability in the second phase of adolescence, the disequilibrium nevertheless continues. Consequently the opportunity for inner change continues, but now with the help of thoughtful reflection and planned experimentation.

One of the unique characteristics of adolescence, in both phases, is the recurrent alternation of episodes of disturbed behavior with periods of relative quiescence. These episodes have the qualities both of rebellion and experiment. There are times when the instinctual drives and needs gain ascendancy over the ego and superego controls. As a result there is often a temporary and essentially normal outburst of more primitive behavior. Presently the instinctual drives are again brought under control, the tensions relieved, and the balance of forces restored. During the resulting period of quiescence there is the opportunity for working over what has happened, and the ego gains additional strength through the mastery of the new experience.

These episodes and the ensuing periods of calm may last only a few minutes or hours, or may extend over a period of months. An episode of brief duration is illustrated by a reaction in a 15-year-old boy who normally was very shy and afraid to reveal his feelings. He had been attracted to a girl for some time, and under the influence of feelings of warmth and excitement at a New Year's Eve party he confessed to her that he loved her. When she did not take his statement seriously, he felt hurt, became morose, and vowed that he would never again love any girl. The next day, however, he realized that the girl could not have been expected to think he was serious and he then decided to ask her for a date.

An episode of longer duration is exemplified by the experience of an 18-year-old girl who on her own initiative went on a summer-long European trip, her first prolonged separation from her parents. Under what were very free and unsupervised circumstances, she yielded to her impulses and joined the other girls of her group in "wild" behavior which included drinking to the point of intoxication. She had sexual relations with a man whom she hardly knew and felt quite guilty and remorseful. Upon returning home she announced that she had decided to spend the next summer vacation with her family. During the school year she had a steady boy friend and behaved very conservatively, steering clear of both alcohol and sex. Off and on throughout the year she reflected on the experiences of her summer in Europe. As her guilt feelings lessened she came to recognize a cause-and-effect relationship between what had been an excessive conformity and dependency and her exaggerated, rebellious behavior of the previous summer. By the end of the following summer vacation she was able to assume responsibility for herself, her standards, and her behavior in a quite mature way.

THE OFFSET

Adolescence comes to an end when the psychological disequilibrium of the second phase is replaced by a relatively stable equilibrium. Adolescence as a stage of development ends at this point regardless of whether the patterns which crystallize into the final equilibrium are adaptive or maladaptive. From the viewpoint of personality structure, the adolescent will have achieved a reasonable balance between the ego, id, and superego. Ideally, the superego facilitates adaptation to social reality without excessive prohibition of the instinctual needs, and the ego is able to control the instinctual drives while still having ready access to their energy and creative potential.

The adolescent struggle may also be resolved, however, by pathological means. Some individuals pass through these years with a minimum of upheaval. They maintain a status quo in which the id is dominated by a rigid ego-superego alliance, this in turn sometimes being supported by excessively controlling parents. Such youngsters are often considered to be "very good" and may be held up to other teenagers as the ideal model. They have not experienced the constructive changes which normally occur in adolescence. Though adult in years, they are emotionally immature.

Other individuals experience what has been described as "protracted" adolescence. The offset is markedly delayed because the conflicts and behavior typical of adolescence persist and become "a way of life." Protracted adolescence usually does terminate, but in some cases it continues indefinitely.

In many instances, the offset of adolescence may come about through the establishment of a neurosis, a character disorder, or a borderline psychotic disorder. The equilibrium thus achieved, while sometimes quite stable, is easily threatened and much psychic energy may be required to maintain it. The consequence of such illnesses is a decreased flexibility, adaptability, and productivity. Adolescence, nevertheless, is over.

It must be emphasized that the shift from disequilibrium to equilibrium as marking the transition between adolescence and adulthood is only a relative distinction. The balance between intrapsychic forces may seldom again be as unstable as in adolescence, but neither will it ever be completely stable. The normal state is not one of stasis but of dynamic tension which permits spontaneity, creativity, and flexibility in coping with the challenges to be faced in adult life.

The physiological changes of puberty which initiate adolescence stabilize somewhere in the mid-teens. This usually occurs long before there is an equivalent balancing out of the emotional and psychological responses. It may be said, then, that adolescence as a stage of human development has a biological onset and a psychological offset.

Early Adolescence

In early adolescence those features of behavior characteristic of preadolescence are still in evidence and even more marked. The increased activity, increased aggressiveness, decreased dependence upon the adult (especially parental) world, and the greater scope of social interaction continue to mount with no sharp demarcation between preadolescence and adolescence.

THE IMPACT OF PUBERTY

The most evident sign of transition is the burgeoning physical maturation caused by the marked increase in sex-specific hormones (see Chapter 1). The bodily changes, so noticeable to others, are also a source of the most intense preoccupation for the pubescent youngster. The spurt in general body growth, the increase in size of the genital organs, and the gradual appearance of secondary sex characteristics are both longed for and feared. Similarly, the appearance of menstruation in the girl and ejaculation in the boy, and of a biologically mature capacity for orgasm in both sexes, causes apprehension but at the same time carries the exciting promise of adult functioning. The changes of puberty stimulate and necessitate new responses on the part of the adolescent and his environment.

With the advent of full puberty, the repressed sexual interest in the parents, the repressed incestuous wishes and related fantasies now press strongly toward consciousness. These impulses, if not checked intrapsychically, would result in a frank sexual feeling toward the parents. It is here that the superego and the incest taboo of earlier development come to bear. As a rule these impulses are blocked before they can become conscious, a host of ego defenses being marshaled to keep them in check. For example, youngsters now show a marked increase in modesty and usually forbid father or mother to be in the room when they dress; they may find parental jokes with sexual implications offensive or disgusting; parental tastes and appearance are viewed as drab and old-fashioned; and the parents tend to be written off as uninteresting and uncongenial. Frequently the best efforts that the ego can muster are insufficient in the face of the strength of the urges; the temptation toward erotic interest in the parents continues to threaten. The boy may catch a glimpse of his mother bathing, or the girl may see her father undressing, and suddenly unwanted thoughts are pressing for attention. The youngster may erupt "for no reason at all" and become hard to live with. As the tension resulting from inner conflict increases, the id-ego-superego balance is disturbed, and the ego is hard-pressed in its efforts at simultaneously maintaining the internal equilibrium and a good relationship with the outer world.

In early adolescence, the ego responds to the surge of sexual and aggressive energies as though it were both a liability and an asset. It is a source of anxiety because it provides impetus for carrying sexual and aggressive urges into action. On the other hand, the increase in energy is an asset because it also is available to the ego for constructive and integrative purposes, and it contributes to the great resiliency and recuperative capacity of the adolescent.

The pubertal surge frequently is met first by an attempt to shore up the existing defenses. In its attempt to cope, the ego may employ any or all of the defensive and adaptive techniques acquired during the previous stages of development. A particular defense may be used tenaciously for a period of time before yielding to another, or different defenses may be employed one after another in rapid succession so that the adolescent's behavior appears erratic.

A pubertal boy may suddenly become possessed by a passionate interest in some hobby that had previously interested him only slightly. For example, he eats, drinks, and sleeps model cars and develops an active if limited social life with others who share this same interest. His parents note that they seldom see him any more: he spends all of his free time in the basement workshop or at his friends' houses. Or, the reverse situation may occur. A youngster who has had a well-developed and stable pattern of school performance and hobbies becomes bored and dissatisfied with everything and complains constantly. The boredom, however, is only a defense against his strong internal conflict and tension, and he suddenly may throw himself into a new activity only to decide that it is stupid and shift to something else.

THE MOVE TOWARD INDEPENDENCE

Sooner or later the adolescent seeks to solve his dilemma by a partial but significant withdrawal from the emotional relationship with the parents. This maneuver initiates a series of changes that are both disturbing and necessary to development toward adulthood. There is less dependence on parents and less acceptance of their emotional support. There is a decrease in the influence of parental attitudes and values, both as currently expressed and as internalized during earlier development through identification with the parents. In consequence, at a time when the young person is greatly in need of help, he loses a significant measure of support. Because his view of himself and the world has been determined largely by the stability of his relationship with his parents, he now feels threatened and confused.

Most importantly, though, the loosening of old ties also provides the opportunity to revise those defensive and adaptive patterns which, while appropriate in childhood, are not well suited to adult functioning. With the diminution in the influence of former identifications, a re-evaluation, a reality-testing of the parents and their attitudes, follows. There is the possibility, then, for desirable change in personality as a part of normal adolescent development. During the latency stage, children pretty much take for granted the parents' judgments about who are "nice" people and who are not, but in puberty they begin to question these judgments and characteristically strike up relationships with persons disapproved of by the parents. This is helpful to the adolescent not only in attaining some distance from the parents but also in providing a chance to weigh and test out what was previously accepted without question. There is the example of the girl from a "nice home" who appears to swing all the way over and insists on her right to run with the "hippies." More likely than not, she will court contacts of this kind only temporarily and then decide that she doesn't really feel comfortable with them—but, importantly, this now is her own decision based on her own experience. Some adolescents live "double lives" while they attempt to reconcile the old attitudes with the new perceptions. Note, for example, the boy who is able to "con" his parents and other adults into seeing him as a "nice" boy, but who is known to his peers as a "kook"; or the obverse case of the boy whose parents see him as a "kook," but who is regarded by his peers as a "square."

EARLY ADOLESCENCE

The withdrawal from the parents normally causes a kind of mourning reaction or episodes of depression in the adolescent. Psychologically this is similar to mourning the actual loss of a loved person. Since the parents in fact are present, however, the cause of the depression is obscure to both the adolescent and his parents and is likely to be labeled simply as "moodiness." The engendered feelings of loneliness and isolation can stir up an intense desire for self-gratification, which then leads to increased eating or to masturbation. These activities in turn are likely to be followed by attitudes of self-condemnation and despair which increase the feelings of depression. A compensatory reaction is evidenced in moods of elation and exaltation attendant upon the finding of new love objects. In large measure, the mood swings of adolescents are directly related to the making and breaking of relationships, whether in actuality or only in their fantasies.

Unable to remain closely dependent upon his parents, and considerably distressed emotionally, the adolescent sometimes reacts to his internal disruption with the fear that he is going crazy. He is desperately in need of new supportive relationships and turns to others outside the immediate family for limits on his behavior, for guidance, and for identification. He forms transient but often intense attachments and "crushes" upon a variety of adults, such as teachers, coaches, and camp counselors. With some of these individuals he has a genuine relationship. With others, such as celebrities who are admired from a distance, the relationship exists in fantasy. In these identifications there is a "trying on for size" of many different modes of behavior, attitudes, and values. In each trial identity the youngster's individuality is further delineated by the discovery of some modes that seem to suit him and others that are alien.

Relationships with adults nevertheless are also perceived as potentially dangerous. This is due to a fear of losing one's individuality and identity. The very attraction to and closeness with an admired adult pose the threat that the latter's firmly established and stronger identity will overwhelm and subordinate the tentative, undefined identity of the adolescent. Besides, the adolescent's relationship to any adult contains the residua of still unresolved yearnings toward and conflicts with the parents. The new relationship often is precipitously forsaken by the adolescent, to the surprise, hurt, and bewilderment of the "idol."

Withdrawal from the parents commonly is facilitated by derogation of them: nothing they say or do is acceptable or even worthy of consideration. Childlike obedience to parental wishes and standards is totally at odds with the establishment of individuality. Some adolescents rebel and fairly readily become independent of their parents; some withdraw with great difficulty, though they do struggle against their attachment to them; and some remain dependent and tied to the family while creating an illusion of independence by behaving negativistically, turning love into hate and admiration into contempt. The adolescent is not single-minded, then, in his withdrawal from his parents and his attempts to sever parental ties and dependency. He also desperately needs his parents and wants their love and care, and is often reluctant to assume independence and its responsibilities. The regressive urge to resolve conflicts of puberty by returning to the remembered comforts of childhood contends for a long time with the progressive but frightening need to break parental ties.

For all these reasons the early adolescent's behavior at home often is turbulent, with recurrent periods of negativism and rebellion, followed by intervals of pleasantness and cooperation. The girl who provokes a violent family scene in the afternoon, demanding that she be allowed to single-date boys in cars, may want her parents to tuck her in bed and kiss her good night that same night. At first the rebellion tends to be primarily verbal. With repeated self-assertion, however, the adolescent's effort to achieve independence tends to take the form of action, at times rebellious and at times constructive.

THE PEER GROUP

In the transition from childhood to adulthood, the adolescent finds a temporary way station with others of his kind. The peer group provides a sense of belonging and a feeling of strength and power that is very important to him. In order to gain acceptance by the group the youngster often tends to conform completely in modes of dress, hair style, musical taste, and the like. The peer group, greatly expanded by modern means of transportation and communication, today constitutes an adolescent "culture" which has its own language, customs, social institutions, modes and methods of solving problems, and philosophies (see Chapter 2). Discussion of all the traits of this "culture" is a potentially endless task, but some examples will illustrate the role of the dynamic forces shaping their form and function.

Adolescence is a period in which telephoning and dancing are prominent. It is evident that both of these activities are associated with the pressure toward love relationships, and both indeed display the need for compromise that is the hallmark of boy-girl relationships in early adolescence. A boy or girl talking on the phone may engage in a variety of body postures and contortions: head down, feet up; lying on the floor; climbing and draping one's self around an easy chair; or taut upright attention. The twisting and squirming has an erotic quality to it. The conversation itself varies greatly. It may consist of a constant "repartee" in which all sorts of remarks with double meanings are exchanged, or an endless account of activities during the day. Gossip is shared; counsel is asked for and received; dates are planned, made, and broken; and various details of personal-social experience are discussed. The amount of time involved is truly extraordinary, and often is measured in hours rather than minutes.

The telephone is an ideal instrument for simultaneous physical distance and erotic proximity. One has a voice speaking intimately into one's ear and an ear at one's lips, and yet there are no possible complications if control over sexual feelings relaxes a little. In addition, the telephone provides the adolescent with a wonderful means of fulfilling the need for flight from his parents to his peers without ever leaving the home. Dial-a-peer and he is transferred out of one world and into the other, escaping too close family involvement by turning to others in the same predicament.

Dancing has occupied a central place in the customs of many cultures. The rhythmic bodily activity of dancing satisfies a number of needs. There is the delight in physical movement for its own sake, and the feeling of release which comes with the discharge of the tensions in activity. On the other hand, dancing provides a means of expressing more specific sexual and aggressive urges both in symbolic form and in action. Dancing can be an aphrodisiac, a part of the foreplay that is the first step toward sexual union. In the adolescent "culture" dancing can serve any or all of the purposes stated above. But dancing offers the youngster incomplete discharge of sexual tension. This is one reason why the forms or "styles" of dance are constantly changing, one dancing fad displacing another sometimes with bewildering rapidity. In a way, all forms of dancing involving both sexes approach the goal of sexual gratification, whether or not it is reached.

Moreover, for most teenagers it is important that this goal should not be reached. Early adolescents in particular are not ready for coitus and need to mobilize defenses against too much sexual stimulation at the same time that they seek to express sexual feelings. Just as the telephone is an instrument of compromise, most dancing also affords a means of merging drive and defense. Many current dances have an unusually overt sexual quality to their movements. The rolling of the pelvis, the thrusting of the hips, and the thigh movements all are grossly and unmistakably erotic. At the same time, the "rules" of these dances require that the dancers seldom touch and never embrace each other. Sexual urges can be expressed and coitus can be symbolically enacted, but the youngsters are protected from the danger of close physical contact.

There are many other phenomena which could be discussed. For example, adolescent speech with its striving for difference, for uniqueness, and for an additional edge of stimulation and excitement; adolescent clothing and hair styling with its quality of novelty and exhibition; and adolescent letter writing and composition of poetry. A great variety of forms express the intense need of adolescents to love but to avoid excessive stimulation; to separate and differentiate from the parents but to find adequate controls; to regard themselves as unique but to be enveloped by the peer group; to express and show themselves to the world but to keep a secret and personal "inner space" inviolate.

MASTURBATION

Masturbation becomes a central concern in early adolescence, generally more so for boys than for girls. However, those adolescent girls who do masturbate regularly are prone to feel as much guilt and anxiety as do boys. Girls may be more secretive than boys because of greater feelings of shame, but children of both sexes feel intensely conflicted about masturbation, both consciously and unconsciously. Our culture has been rife with rumor regarding the harmful consequences of masturbation, and these rumors are given credibility by parental attitudes which on the whole have been disapproving and prohibitive of sexuality. In addition, children generate their own fears and false ideas about masturbation. With the increase in masturbatory activity which begins at puberty, the old fantasies from earlier stages of development are revived to complicate the new, age-appropriate fantasies and intensify the conflict and guilt feelings.

The revived incestuous feelings and the associated fear of retaliatory castration tend to cause a hypochondriacal preoccupation with the genitalia. Adolescent boys are much concerned with the discharge of seminal fluid and construct their own fantasies about its significance. They watch anxiously for signs of damage following masturbatory activity. The discharge of seminal fluid following ejaculation may not be understood as a normal phenomenon, or its leakage in association with sexual excitement may be taken as a sign that "something is wrong with the valves inside the penis." Ejaculation may be perceived as an irreparable draining of virility, a using up of one's finite masculinity and reproductive capacity. If the sexual and aggressive urges are confusingly intertwined, the ejaculate may even be regarded as a dangerous and destructive poison. The normal pubertal increase in the size of the penis and testicles sometimes is falsely attributed to too much "handling" of these organs, and is regarded as evidence of damage. The opposite belief that the genitals are too small and will never reach full masculine size also may be attributed to masturbation. The ultimate consequence of damage from masturbation often is conceived to be a premature loss of sexual potency. Girls similarly imagine all kinds of dire consequences from masturbation. Among them are premature sterility, defective genitalia, and loss of value as a marriage partner. Normal vaginal discharge may be regarded with great concern as a proof of having harmed oneself.

As was suggested above, sexual and aggressive elements can be confusingly admixed in masturbatory fantasies. Thus sexual fantasies can be tinged with violence, and aggressive fantasies can cause sexual excitement. This admixture or fusion accounts in large measure for the relative, and sometimes complete, absence of tenderness as a component in the sexual play and fantasies during early adolescence.

All of the various imagined consequences of masturbation can be seen to stem from the fear of castration. This fear is reinforced by the carry-over from early childhood of the belief that parents are all-knowing. There is the concern that forbidden sexual activity will in some way become known to the world. The adolescent worries that his shameful secret is revealed by his acne, by the bulge of a spontaneous erection, a shiftiness of his eyes, or his staying too long in the bathroom. He fears that he is being silently condemned, and his expectation of derision and humiliation helps explain the excessive embarrassment, self-consciousness, withdrawal, and self-depreciation so often observed in early adolescents. On the other hand, guilt and fear can be denied and defended by behavior such as exhibitionistic dress and excessive forwardness, and by boastfulness to one's peers of masturbatory prowess.

All this notwithstanding, masturbation is an essentially normal activity. It is a normal response to increased sexual development, and is necessary to the control and integration of new urges and to the working out of new relationships through trial acting in fantasy. It serves as a means of experimenting with new biological capacities, a reassurance against castration anxiety simply because the organ is still there and functioning, and a temporary retreat from the increased problems in relationships with people. It may also be used for relieving tensions both sexual and nonsexual in origin. Either excessive masturbation or complete abstention from it can be symptomatic of underlying psychopathology deserving of evaluation, but masturbation in itself is not a cause of primary mental disorder. Yet, even when youngsters have been told about the normal nature of masturbation, their fantasies, feelings, and worries about self-harm may cause them considerable distress.

The way in which the adolescent experiments with orgasm as the climax to masturbation illustrates how masturbation can serve normal development. The adolescent learns that sexual excitement and engorgement and erection of the penis or the clitoris can be initiated at will, and that orgastic climax with the ensuing predictable subsidence of tension can be quickly brought about or repeatedly deferred by the manner of masturbation. This contributes to a developing sense of mastery over the sexual impulses and the new sexual capacities, and helps the adolescent prepare for heterosexual relationships. In the male, the prominence of the erection, the forcefulness of the ejaculation, and the tangibility of the ejaculate may also foster acceptance of the masculine, aggressive role in relationships with girls.

MENSTRUATION

Menstruation is, of course, the exclusive feature of female puberty. It serves both as a stimulus and focal point for fantasies about what it means to become a woman. Some girls may unconsciously perceive menstrual "bleeding" as a proof of injury (an extension of the earlier concern about not having a penis). They may react to menstruation with feelings of revulsion or with depression, temporarily refusing to face and accept it for what it is, namely, a very tangible proof of femaleness. Because of the "bleeding," the menses also may reawaken fearful childhood fantasies in which sexual intercourse was imagined to be an act of violence, thereby causing excessive fear of heterosexuality. Or the menses in some girls may reinforce an earlier repudiation of the female genitals as being filthy and smelly, because of their proximity to the organs of elimination.

On the other hand, menstruation heralds the potential for pregnancy and child-bearing, thereby facilitating identification with adult women in a healthy and positive way. Girls who have had little conflict about their femininity in earlier childhood usually accept menstruation for its positive implications.

It has been suggested that menstruation may serve as an organizing force in the mental and emotional functioning of women. Prior to its advent the effects of hormonal fluctuations are unpredictable, unsettling, sometimes only vaguely perceived, and distractingly nonspecific. And the girl often is correspondingly vague, scattered, and disorganized. She may be a rebellious complainer who is generally unable to explain her disquietude to herself or others. Therefore menstruation, as a specific event with a clearly observable beginning and ending and a definite set of sensations, occurring with increasing regularity and predictability, provides a stimulus and a focus for further development and maturation. Following the onset of menstruation girls tend to become more organized and logical in their thought processes and behavior, and more effective in expressing themselves than in preadolescence. It is difficult to verify such a close correlation between endocrine and psychic function but the hypothesis merits consideration.

Normally the major effect of menstruation is to provide impetus toward the full acceptance of femininity. The aggressiveness in relationships with boys, so characteristic of preadolescence, gives way to qualities of softness, shyness, and passivity. The girl begins to show acceptance of the aggressive role of the male and becomes more inviting and receptive in her attitudes toward him.

THE NEW BODY AND SELF IMAGE

All the changes in the body, not only in sexual development and function but also in physical size and strength, necessitate modification of the earlier established mental images of the body. The recognition and acceptance of what one is, physically and biologically, is a prerequisite for the successful achievement of a mature personal identity. The girl, for example, must accept and integrate the realities of menstruation, breast development, and broadening of the hips. The boy must integrate the various changes in his physical self and his considerable increase in physical strength. The latter has a constructive but also a destructive potential, and often is a source of anxiety in interpersonal relationships, since aggressive urges that formerly were expressed mainly in fantasy now could be carried out in reality. In many cases, for example, the boy realizes that if it actually came to a fight he well might be able to win out over his father.

The development of a body image and identity acceptable to the adolescent may be impaired, however, by normal, unavoidable variations from the prevailing cultural stereotype of masculinity and femininity. Unusual muscular development and a flat chest may trouble the girl, and pudginess or a high voice may trouble the boy. Body image also may fail to evolve appropriately because of the previously discussed unconscious fantasies and conflicts about one's sexual anatomy and functions, which may still be unresolved.

ACTION AND IMPULSIVE BEHAVIOR

In early adolescence in particular, relief from tensions associated with the pressures from the instinctual drives may be sought in action, often in the form of impulsive behavior. The meaning of this behavior in normal adolescence and whether it serves a constructive purpose are not entirely clear. As was noted earlier, there is an excess of physical energy at this time, and this feeds into the need for vigorous activity as a part of healthy development. Action can be a normal means of relief from tension and anxiety. Even impulsive behavior may serve important constructive purposes in seeking the limits of external controls, in testing reality, and in the search for identity in "measuring" oneself against others. As such it can help to integrate new abilities into the array of adaptive skills. The gaining of mastery over the expression of impulses is not merely the inhibition of expression, however; it is more the rechanneling of inner drives toward useful and constructive outlets. Some expression of impulses in action is necessary if such new channels are to be found. The Duke of Wellington's observation that the Battle of Waterloo was won on the playing fields of Eton made just this point: by mastering and integrating action patterns in sports, character was built; courage, endurance, and effective aggressive qualities were enhanced; and mastery of impulses was achieved.

In some adolescents, however, action serves not to reduce anxiety to a manageable level but rather to avoid having to endure it at all. Action is a means of evading rather than facing and resolving the underlying conflicts. Such repetitious action is an acting out of unconscious conflicts and is indeed symptomatic and a serious impediment to maturation. Action or activity for its own sake may even come to predominate in the life of an adolescent, interfering directly with intellectual development and learning.

Action that follows thought, that translates a plan into reality, aids development and adaptation. The opposite is true of action that substitutes for thought, that gives the impulse quick expression before thought can intervene. For example, the 14-year-old boy who plans, builds, and flies an engine-driven model airplane has a chance to evaluate the effectiveness of both his thought and his action, quite the opposite of his contemporary who spends all his free time "hacking around," constantly on the move.

THE CAPACITY FOR THOUGHT

The capacity for the highest level of abstract thinking first makes its appearance at puberty. This is a development of unique importance. The ability to reason inductively and deductively at an abstract level provides the adolescent with important new adaptive and defensive techniques. It is now possible to deal with problems through trial action in the mind's eye, considering alternative plans for their solution before taking action in reality. Besides, the greater intellectual capacities contribute to the blossoming of interests, abilities, and activities in the arts, sciences, humanities, and philosophy. For a time such burgeoning interest may yield little fruit; the youth is still too preoccupied with himself to be able to offer much to the outside world. At times, thinking turns into complicated intellectualization, primarily concerned with defending oneself against the inner claims of the sexual and aggressive drives, and the original aim of problem solving thus is diverted.

The capacity for abstract thinking, although phase-specific and characteristic, nevertheless varies a good deal from one adolescent to another. For example, some adolescents are able to think with ease, using only mental abstractions; others lean heavily on written or diagrammatic presentation; and still others require presentation in three dimensions, as, for example, the boy who devises a complex and remarkable apparatus by the trial-and-error method, using component parts. Still others display their intellectual ability in even more tangible and practical terms—as in raising and experimenting with animals or developing a successful small business enterprise.

BOY-GIRL RELATIONSHIPS

Throughout the turmoil of early adolescence the youngster is constantly concerned with the all-important task of achieving a healthy relationship with a member of the opposite sex.

In spite of the conflicts and anxieties stirred up by the impact of puberty, there is a consuming interest in everything sexual. And this interest is expressed in diverse ways, many of which do not require actual physical relationship. There is, for example, an intense curiosity and an avid pursuit of all possible sources of information about sex. Many a child's first acquaintance with the encyclopedia results from the persistent rumor that there is detailed sexual information in it, if only it can be found. Conversations between adolescents frequently are overwhelmingly and frankly sexual, and at other times more in symbolic form with much play on words with double meaning. There is a more or less constant preoccupation with heterosexual daydreams and masturbatory fantasies, although these at first are likely to be highly romanticized and sparse in details about the imagined sexual activities.

As has been stated previously, there also is an initial retreat to the safety of association with members of one's own sex. In this association, sexual activity and experimentation are likely to occur both between individuals and in groups. Among boys, mutual masturbation and group masturbation are quite common, and episodes of anal intercourse and oral-genital contact (fellatio) are not rare. Analogous behavior among girls may range from hand-holding and kissing to breast fondling and mutual masturbation. It is important to recognize that such behavior at this age does not necessarily lead to sexual deviation in adulthood. This is not a clinically significant homosexuality and should not be so labeled. At this age homosexual behavior more appropriately should be viewed as a temporary defense against the fears associated with the move toward full heterosexual relationships.

Again, a gauche aggressive technique is used to cope with the first anxiety-laden contacts with the opposite sex. Verbal interchange is bantering and teasing in nature, and may become quite openly derogatory if the threat of closeness is too intense. Physical sexual urges are expressed in disguised form through body-contact games and playful roughhousing. Frequently aggression and sexuality become so intertwined that aggressively tinged sex play and sexually tinged fighting are indistinguishable. This kind of behavior is quite common, even between an adolescent brother and sister, a form of interaction that parents find particularly upsetting.

This most typical picture is only one of a wide range of possible patterns of behavior. As was mentioned earlier, some children are so threatened by their instincts that they try to curb all expression of sexuality and persist in the behavior of latency. Others attempt to cope with puberty by stifling it, rigidly controlling sexual feelings and avoiding any sort of activity with either sex. In essence they defend against puberty with asceticism, denying the very existence of their sexual urges. Still others seemingly have little conflict over sexuality and welcome the opportunity to begin dating. In some cases the "boy-crazy" girl may be rushing ahead in an attempt to overcome her fears, but often she may merely be able to accept her sexuality at an earlier date than can her peers.

THE RESOLUTION OF EARLY ADOLESCENCE

As his ego begins to cope with, assimilate, and integrate the changes brought about by puberty, the adolescent turns increasingly toward the opposite sex. Trial behavior through fantasy has served as a preparation; fantasies and activities shared with others of the same sex have given reassurance that the fascination and desire are normal; awareness of a similar interest and readiness on the part of members of the opposite sex has reduced shyness. Dating begins, and by the end of early adolescence heterosexual dating usually has become established.

During the earliest phases of dating sexuality may sometimes be crude. The intense curiosity and the still persistent fears result in experimentation barely tempered by affection or tenderness. At the same time, there is still a considerable admixture of aggression and sex. While sexual intercourse is not common during this often frantic first stage of learning about mature sexual functioning, the greatest preoccupation nevertheless is with the physical aspects of sex rather than the emotional relationship. The implications of sexual maturity are tested out with the aim of learning about one's own sexual role and determining its acceptability to the opposite sex. In general, the heterosexual relationships of early adolescence are characterized more by experimentation than by genuine emotional involvement.

MAJOR CHARACTERISTICS OF EARLY ADOLESCENCE

During early adolescence the youngster becomes acquainted with and accepts a remarkably changed body, achieves a definitive separation and differentiation of the new self from the parents, and experiments with new kinds of relationships with peers of both sexes. More specifically, the major characteristics of this phase of adolescent development are as follows:

1. Rebellion against and withdrawal from adults and their values. Initially the rebellion is mainly verbal, but it becomes more action-oriented as adolescence progresses. The detachment from parents is impelled by guilt over the oedipal fantasies reawakened now in the threatening context of near-adult capabilities for sexual and aggressive behavior, and by the need to discover individual identity, which is felt to be jeopardized by too close an attachment to the adult with his strongly established identity. The need for guidance from adults and for adult models for identification persists, but attachments even to adults other than the parents usually are transitory.

2. Intense narcissism, with a strong preoccupation with one's own body and self.

3. The peer group is of vital importance, serving as a way station during the transition from childhood to adulthood.

4. Sexual urges and feelings become intense and gain expression, at first in fantasies and then in masturbatory and other sexual activity as the adolescent moves into beginning heterosexual relationships.

5. Marked increase in aggressive urges, now supported by a corresponding increase in physical size and strength.

6. Marked increase in emotional and intellectual capabilities with a parallel broadening of interests and activities.

7. Attitudes and behavior in general are characterized by unpredictable changes and much experimentation.

Late Adolescence

As the young person moves from early to late adolescence, adults respond to his growth and increasing maturity and begin to expect him to assume a definitive role in society. During the early teens his pseudo-adult behavior, while often disturbing to adults, tends to be regarded with amused indulgence like that accorded the young child. During his late adolescence, however, in the latter years of high school and the undergraduate college years, society expects him to get down to business.

As they become still more independent of their families, the young man and the young woman become more closely involved with society at large; and society, in turn, begins to encounter them, taking their measure, attempting to shape them, and at the same time adapting to them. Adolescents now begin to hold jobs; unemployment becomes a problem; they have an influence on politics; they do volunteer work in hospitals; they pose a threat on the streets; they appear as offenders in juvenile court.

Certain social structures have been developed to cope with these emerging adults. Some of these cultural institutions seem to have a defensive role: adolescents are not to grow up too fast, "Let them season a bit and learn the ropes." As has been stated, a minimal driving age exists, with automobile insurance to pay; there is a minimum age for seeing adult films and for drinking in a bar; and signatures are not legally binding until age 21. Also, there are the implicit, and sometimes explicit, social conventions such as: Do you shave? Is your hair properly cut? Is your style of dress right? Appearance can have a lot to do with acceptability for employment, or as a suitor from the viewpoint of a girl's parents, or how a policeman is likely to treat the young person. His past performance "record" suddenly becomes crucial: academic standing, behavior, athletics, encounters with the law, and reputation in general (in terms of kind of recommendations that he can get). The past catches up as the world begins to consider and judge, approving or disapproving.

Adolescents are enormously aware of these realities. At the high-school age, some of them respond by striving for all the plaudits and plus marks they can get: they graduate from high school with honors; they become Eagle scouts; they become three-letter men in sports; they earn money during summer vacations; they win national merit scholarships. Others respond with a point-by-point rejection of social expectations: their hair is too long and unkempt; their clothes are provocative and often dirty; and their school performance is spotty and uncertain or they may have dropped out.

At the college age some adolescents go through a rather extreme phase: boys grow beards and girls wear long stockings of every hue and texture; their social life may include guitars and marihuana or LSD; their sex life may be both active and chaotic; they live "around," in and out of their own and their friends' homes; scholastic achievement may range from brilliant to abysmal, depending upon their interest in a given subject; they tend to be very casual about money, borrowing from one another, hocking expensive birthday gifts, or appropriating money from their parents in what amounts to stealing. Often they are involved in some sort of protest movement, be it for academic freedom, civil rights, or legalizing the use of marihuana.

Both the conforming and the nonconforming adolescents are responding to the same set of social realities, and each type tries to master them in its own way, one by beating the "establishment" at its own game, the other by refusing to play.

Society has a vested interest in trying to initiate its youth into approved adult patterns. Apprenticeship training, compulsory education, driver training, the Boy Scouts, ROTC, "young" political clubs, and religious organizations for youth are dedicated in part to integrating youngsters into society. "Good citizenship" is the goal. More recently, the Peace Corps, the Job Corps, and the antipoverty programs are also in part pointed toward such "cultural facilitation"—helping the new young adults develop a sense of belonging, of being needed, of feeling that a role exists for them that "means something."

One of the hazards for the adolescent at this time of life is growing up toward adulthood and finding that he is "on the outside looking in," that nobody seems to need or want him, nobody cares whether he is there or not, that there is no niche for him to fill, no place for him. There is the danger that some youngsters will slide into some sort of limbo; currently, this comes under the heading of "alienation."

Alienation is a complex issue and much concern has been engendered by the recognition that it exists. It seems to be highly prevalent and plainly stereotyped; groups of girls and boys look, act, and speak alike, know one another, and hang out together at the same coffee house or city park. It is possible, however, that this phenomenon may be only the current version of a perennial problem: adolescent uncertainty garbing itself in arrogance and super-certainty, and using that easiest way of seeming to be an individual—to be "against." For it is difficult to be truly individual and unique, and it can be lonely, frightening, and dangerous.

Young people want to be something more than "puppets" who do what they are told, more than good boys and girls who conform and have no individuality. They want to be persons in their own right. But just who can they be, and just what can they do? For youngsters with unusual talents or intellectual gifts, the opportunities are many; but for others, doors are closed and the search for the self seems to be hemmed in at every point by a multitude of requirements and by incessant requests to conform. These youngsters may seek an easy out by banding together to attack the conventions, challenge the standards, and flout the values of the larger society. They form a "society" of their own wherein the emphasis is on the needs of adolescents rather than the needs of adults—a caricature of the larger society.

One of the striking characteristics of this time of life is the continuation of the sense of play. Young people have not yet attained full adulthood, and in a very real sense they "play" at being adult. It doesn't really count, it's "not for real." There is a sense of saying and doing serious things which somehow are not really serious. Experiences are intense, emotional, and real—and yet they are not quite hard reality. Reality is felt to be reversible and one's acts forgiveable; a sense of permanency is lacking. The time sense is distorted, with strong feelings of impatience and a desire for immediacy.

Like young children adolescents live very much in the here and now, and to adult eyes they sometimes seem almost idiotically unaware of the potential seriousness of many of their actions—and the adult is not necessarily wrong: dropping out of school often means economic suicide and a constricted adult life; sexual promiscuity can lead to unwanted pregnancies and to too early marriage; playing "chicken" with high-powered automobiles can kill people; taking drugs can be ruinous.

Society tends to react to the nonconformist, and he may be dealt with in a brusque way which often has a quality of retaliation. The message is: "Shape up or ship out." The earliest and commonest form of such exclusion is usually encountered at school: conform or be suspended. Drivers' licenses are granted and retracted and insurance rates are raised with a similar message. There are pressures on the adolescent to disengage himself from a particular group or friendship as soon as the nonconformist pattern appears. On the other hand, in being accepted into an adult-approved group, the message once again is: "Conform or else." To these young people, society appears to function as a screening device which includes some and excludes others.

At present, in prosperous North America, adolescents are given many of the economic privileges which in the past were earned through years of hard work. Their privileges exist without accompanying responsibilities, and they are in the position of young princes with a world of pleasure created for them. Nowadays, it would seem that it is not the adolescent who envies the adult, but the adult who envies the adolescent. The adult may wish to join the colorful, vital, and potent world of the adolescent with its freedom from responsibility. The advertising man knows this very well and everything from soft drinks to automobiles is sold in an aura of adolescent gaiety and sexuality.

In spite of the stresses of adolescence, the vast majority of young people ultimately make an adequate adjustment. The greater number develop their abilities, enter an occupation or profession, get married, have children, and assume the responsibilities and make the commitments to the community which mark the attainment of full adulthood. The "dreams" of adolescence all too frequently tend to be forgotten, perhaps because they are caught in the repression directed at forgetting the painful aspects of these years. When adults later on encounter their own adolescent children, they often show remarkably little understanding of them, and are likely to have little patience with "this adolescent nonsense."

In late adolescence there generally is even less contact with the parents than in early adolescence, with vacillations between independence and dependence and the depression attendant upon the intrapsychic or psychological "loss" of the parents. The fluctuations, however, are less rapid and violent and less extreme. The adolescent finally begins to realize and accept the fact that independence really is available to him. A lower-class youth may hold a job and support himself with his own money; a middle-class youth is likely to be living away from home at college and will often have a summer job or take a cross-country or European trip. These experiences inevitably help to define a sense of independence and competence in caring for oneself. A still further separation from the parents parallels the firm direction of sexual drives toward a specific member of the opposite sex. Young men and women begin to eye one another as potential mates, and marriage looms ahead.

The "loss" of parents now is more real than psychological, and is compensated by more meaningful and mature relationships with one's peers. The previously described intense preoccupation with the self is also relinquished. The revived oedipal conflict is again resolved, but hopefully the rigid superego of childhood now is modified and becomes more reasonable and realistic. This is achieved through a quite conscious process of re-evaluation and acceptance or rejection of the attitudes and values taken in from the parents during earlier development.

LATE ADOLESCENCE

ADOLESCENT LOVE AND THE ROLE OF COITUS

In late adolescence the task shifts from seeking and finding one's sexual identity to exploring it in all its implications. Falling in love now, for the first time, involves feeling a truly intense concern for one's beloved. In the experience of first love, the partner is of paramount importance, this in spite of the fact that first love relationships usually are not long-lasting. Now a quality of tender affection makes its appearance alongside the sexual feelings. In contrast to the self-centered sexual preoccupations and activities of early adolescence, the adolescent now moves toward a shared sexual experience. Mature sexual behavior comprising both tender and sexual feelings for the loved person begins to be demonstrated. Whereas to others the emotions and attitudes of the adolescent who is in love appear sometimes to be exaggerated to the point of caricature, to the adolescent they are exquisitely real.

As has been stated, the impetus of puberty is primarily sexual. The pressure toward sexual relations is imperative and ultimately and almost invariably will prevail. The normal male or female youth becomes biologically ready for coitus, thinks about it, and in due time desires it. Yet for the most part our Western culture (at least in its "official" attitude) disapproves of sexual intercourse outside of marriage. Also, the goal our culture sets for adults—achievement of a firm sexual identity and the union of tender and sexual love in relationships with the marriage partner—is difficult to attain without sexual experience and experimentation during the years of late adolescence.

Our Puritan heritage has burdened us with a set of taboos and prohibitions which historically may have been appropriate but today seem inappropriate in the light of modern understanding and medical scientific advance. In all probability, the forces that originally produced these prohibitions were concerns about venereal disease, illegitimate pregnancy and its destructive impact on the family, and other social values and structures such as property rights and hereditary titles. And underlying these forces were others such as intrafamilial rivalries and the fear of the younger generation which resulted in the need to keep it "down."

But despite the prevailing ethic, the question is: Should adolescents, at an appropriate age, be allowed or perhaps even encouraged to engage in sexual intercourse before marriage? More than that, does such experience foster healthy psychological development and successful adulthood or not?

These are crucial questions. Insofar as our society is concerned with fostering optimum human development and functioning, it needs to face this issue and be willing to consider the effect of sexual relations during adolescence on total development.

Two major and opposing points of view present themselves in our culture. One position regards the sexual mores as outdated. Now that medical science can prevent accidental or unwanted pregnancy, and can provide adequate protection from and treatment for venereal disease, why should the prohibitions be preserved? The argument is that teenagers are biologically, psychologically, and socially ready for sexual intercourse and moreover need this experience to consolidate their sexual identity, sense of self, and pattern of relationships with others. Besides, so vital an aspect of marriage and adult pleasure and love deserves experience and practice. Furthermore, the choice of marital partner and performance as a mate can be arrived at much more intelligently if the sexual factor can be evaluated from the standpoint of personal experience rather than hearsay, forbidden and hedged about by mystery and danger. According to this view, then, it follows that late adolescents, if they act responsibly, should be free to seek coital experience with a variety of partners; that the pleasure-seeking aspect of this kind of behavior should be sanctioned, but with an emphasis on learning and growth; and that protection against pregnancy and possible venereal disease be provided as a matter of course.

The opposing viewpoint differs sharply. Coitus is by no means just another form of pleasure. If its serious and important implications for mature adult relationships are to be fulfilled, it needs some of the prohibitions which our culture has evolved. Above all, it should be concerned with the development of tenderness and affection in heterosexual patterns. Abandonment to sensation-seeking with a variety of partners is no guarantee of growth. Instead, might it not tend to fixate a person on a pleasure-seeking level, delaying development toward mature sexual functioning? This position, while agreeing that to delay sexual experience is stressful, believes that such delay is necessary for full social development. Sexual intercourse is an activity of adulthood, and to turn to it prematurely will by no means ensure the development of sexual and emotional maturity. Moreover, the still present cultural realities are a part of the adolescent's conscience. Youngsters have internalized the cultural prohibitions against premarital sexual relations, and permitting or encouraging them to act in violation of the presumed "norms" will inevitably lead to guilt and serious internal conflicts.

These concerns are for the most part overstated, deriving more from fear of sexual impulses and guilt over sexuality than from careful observation and study. An understanding of the interrelationship between familial-subcultural value systems and individual development makes it clear that the answer to the question under discussion, while it can be generalized, finally has to be formulated in terms of the maturity of a given adolescent boy or girl. The average 13-year-old who is just beginning to feel the effects of puberty is very different from the average 18- or 19-year-old who has established dating patterns and who may already be firmly settled on the road to adult identity. There would probably be fair agreement that coitus in the early teens usually would be "rushing things," and could be dangerous, not only because it might interfere with orderly, sequential development but because of the lack of sufficient maturity to understand and act upon factors such as responsibility to the sexual partner and the possibility of pregnancy. There would be much less of a consensus that the same considerations apply in late adolescence.

Of further significance in any rational consideration of adolescent sexual behavior is the fact that all adolescents do not develop at the same rate. Some 18-year-olds may not be at all ready, developmentally, for sexual intercourse, and may need the help of various cultural attitudes and institutions to reinforce the postponement. Such young people might do well, for example, to go to a non-coeducational college, at least for the first year or two. On the other hand, a 17-year-old or perhaps even younger adolescent from a different family or subcultural background, or because of a constitutionally determined difference in rate of maturation, might well be ready for the experience of sexual relations. Adolescent group pressures may operate to the detriment of some youngsters because the group does not make allowance for differing degrees of individual maturation. In some adolescent groups there is considerable pressure to engage in intercourse in order to be fully accepted by the group. Some members of such groups will pretend to be involved in sexual exploits and thus protect both their status and their mental and emotional equilibrium. But others try to comply, prematurely for themselves, with serious emotional or practical consequences.

Nowadays words like "chastity" and "purity" are heard relatively infrequently in discussions of teenage behavior. Undoubtedly this is related to the widespread cultural acceptance of sex play among adolescents in the form of necking, petting, or "making out"—that is, heterosexual activity short of intercourse, and usually short of orgasm. It also represents a decided shift away from the ideals prevalent in earlier times. Our society seems to be drifting further and further away from the older concepts of morality to some new although still dimly perceived ordering of sex life.

IDENTITY-SEEKING AND IDEALISM

In late adolescence, the signs of identity-seeking are clearly evident. The gradual diminution in the intense preoccupation with self, in combination with the previously discussed loosening of ties to the parents and the internalized parental values, results in an outwardly directed concern with cultural values and ideologies and with social forces. With the capacity to view the parents and society with new objectivity, the failings and hypocrisies seem to stand out with blinding clarity to the adolescent; and at the same time the solutions to social problems seem equally, albeit sometimes naïvely, clear. Everything about the "old" culture is questioned.

Adolescents normally take a serious interest in ethics and religion, as part of the delineation of their own standards and values. A continuous effort is exerted to mediate between instinct and the now uncertain demands of conscience, in the service of forming new ideals and reshaping the conscience to accommodate them. The adolescent shows great concern for the moral probity of parents and other adults and constantly compares words with deeds. Cynicism and feelings of hopelessness alternate with renewed idealism as the repeated discovery of the discrepancy between the ideal and the real necessitates evaluation of the cultural institutions and of one's own values.

With the pubertal surge of the sexual drives, the urge to love expresses itself in many ways. Some of the love feelings are directed to the self, some to people, and some to other objects such as pets, automobiles, books, and scientific projects; and, finally, some of these feelings can seize onto ideas or causes—which then become ideals. Idealization is particularly evident in the feelings for the loved person, who is likely to be regarded as uniquely beautiful, clever, interesting, and noble—indeed, as a perfect individual who is more worthy of love than anyone else in the world. In the case of the automobile, motorcycle, scientific project, or pet animal, the loved object stimulates an intense interest, and is fascinating in every detail. It becomes the focus for much dreaming and planning and a topic of enthusiastic discussion with one's peers.

In order to idealize an idea it of course is necessary that the individual be able to have ideas, to think on an abstract level. And, as was stated earlier, there is a striking increase during puberty in the capacity to abstract, to discern the essential unity, but also the fine distinctions among superficially similar things. The late adolescent has learned to think in concepts; ideas assume a certain solidity for him. They can be weighed, measured, and challenged in one's mind, and be embraced or rejected. Religious and philosophic questions are the object of much thought and discussion; commitment to lengthy, demanding, or even dangerous courses of training is by no means uncommon; and political or humane causes can become a holy grail, the pursuit of which justifies any amount of personal sacrifice, even of one's life.

It is not necessarily the universality of the social value of an idea that determines its appeal for youth. The Hitler "ideal," for example, of building a new, thousand-year "Aryan" empire, regardless of the cost to other peoples, was seized upon by German teenagers in the

1930s with no less zeal and probably in far greater numbers than civil rights and the Negro's cause has been seized upon by young Americans in the mid-1960s.

For the individual young person, the commitment to an ideal also may help to fill the void resulting from increasing independence from the parents. The parents have stood for all kinds of ethical and moral values; they have been the guides and organizers of life. Here is a substitute to fill this void, a nonmaterial substitute which is uncontaminated by sexual elements and does not tempt toward forbidden action.

Important for many—although by no means for all—young idealists is the fact that there are other young people who share one's outlook, a group to which one can belong not so much because of a personal interest in each other, but because of a mutual and "pure" interest in the ideal; love for each other is subordinated to love for "the Cause." Psychologically, this helps the youth to master the still threatening sexual and aggressive feelings and also the problems resulting from the search for identity.

Idealism is one of the most striking characteristics of late adolescence; the idealism of youth is legendary. Zeal, conviction, ardor, and sacrifice are commonplace virtues in the struggle for ideals, and these account in large measure for the fact that a certain amount of cultural change may be stimulated or even initiated by the adolescent.

IDENTITY AND OCCUPATIONAL CHOICE

Inherent in the search for identity is the need to choose one's future occupation. Choice of occupation is determined by all of the relevant influences in a child's life: parental identifications, firmness of sexual identity, capacity to appraise one's talents and abilities, the effect of residual conflicts from early childhood, and the available socio-economic alternatives. At the same time, the selection and pursuit of an occupation also leads to further consolidation of personal and cultural identity.

As an example, the decision of a late adolescent boy to become a physician may have many roots. His relationship with his father included the father's lengthy illness during which the doctor was the one whom the father turned to and obeyed; in becoming a doctor the young man thus becomes someone whom the father listens to and respects. Due to her husband's illness, the mother also had leaned heavily on the doctor; so in becoming a doctor the boy would fulfill unconscious oedipal wishes for closeness with his mother. To him, being a doctor also means activity rather than passivity, and masculine accomplishment, a kind of socially recognized potency. His desire to use his good intellect would be met in this highly professional occupation. The fact that there are substantial social and economic rewards in this profession is also important. And finally, beneath all of this lie forgotten childhood wishes that were never adequately resolved: to see the naked human body and to learn all about it; to hear intimate secrets; to encounter and deal with pain and bleeding.

Such factors, conscious and unconscious, all play a role in determining the adolescent's choice of career.

ATTAINMENT OF ADULT PREROGATIVES

In Western culture the first opportunity for exercising and enjoying adult prerogatives usually comes during late adolescence. The young person is now employable at a fairly reasonable wage, so that financial dependence upon the parents is lessened and in some instances ends. The law permits driving a car, and with the jobs now available to them, many adolescents maintain their own car. Drinking and smoking are common by this time; in some localities adolescents are allowed to drink when they are 18. In these and in other ways, the culture offers them new opportunities to explore and experiment in the adult world.

In this age period where the no-longer-child sometimes and in some ways only "plays" at being adult, the boundary between adolescence and adulthood is at its most fluid and the relations between the two generations is highly conflictual. The adolescent eagerly accepts and even aggressively demands adult prerogatives but strenuously resists the right of adults to control or limit his use of them. On their part, the adults are in a quandary about whether to be permissive and wink at the excesses of adolescents which frequently are dangerous to themselves or others or to hold them strictly accountable in adult terms. But the adolescent appears to be uncompromising in his determination to impose his terms upon the adult culture.

In this widened scope of available activities the late adolescent may feel his independence and identity to be too tenuous to function on a coequal level with adults. Although at times capable of altruism and self-sacrifice, he continues jealously to guard his separateness and autonomy. This aloofness defends as much against his own residual dependency wishes as it does against current influence from adults. It is still primarily his own needs that count. The degree of his defensiveness in this regard reveals whether he has genuinely accomplished the task of separation and independence from his parents. As long as strong dependent emotions can be readily aroused, the old ties are still strong, and the status remains more one of rebellion than of independence.

There is a close bond between narcissistic preoccupation with the self and the continuing search for identity. This is most apparent in the adolescent's use of the newly accessible adult prerogatives. He is more prone to use them as a means of further self-exploration than for their presumably appropriate functions. An adolescent does not drink to relax or to get drunk as much as to discover just what kind of sensations drinking does produce, and, in the process, to master these new experiences. It is only after he has learned about these things that the experiencing of a particular effect of alcohol may become a regular goal of drinking, but this is then an adult use of alcohol.

The phenomena associated with the automobile, particularly in the United States, epitomize this same facet of adolescence. Although the car is greatly prized by the adolescent, this is not only or even primarily because of its utility as a means of transportation. Much of its importance lies in its suitability for expressing and gradually working out inner conflicts, through repeated experimentation. The car can satisfy many needs and have many symbolic meanings.

The automobile can serve the purposes of independence from the parents and adult supervision; of defiance and escape; of mobility and freedom from restraint; of new-found power and action. It provides boundless and self-contained energy, and therefore represents the all important and yet anxiety-creating self-sufficiency which the adolescent is struggling to attain.

The car can also represent the human body: in its external appearances, its lines, its paint job, and its upholstery, it is the image of the body that the adolescent wishes to look at, admire, touch, examine, and even smell; in its mechanics and internal workings it is the body with its inner, hidden functions—here the intense curiosity of the adolescent is sublimated in the "fixing," modifying, tearing down, and reassembling of the car; improvements made in the car, both externally and internally, express the desire to improve one's self.

The automobile further can serve the fantasy life of the adolescent, usually quite unconsciously. It can represent the penis as evidenced, for example, in the pride of ownership and in the preference for a "stick" gearshift which is manipulated repeatedly in the expression, control, and modulation of speed and power. As a symbol of the penis the car is proudly exhibited in a display of color, style, and virility, as it were, in the mating "dance"; or it can be used aggressively against others as a ramming, penetrating weapon. At a regressive level the car can serve to express hostility and contempt in the symbolic "farting" of the exhaust pipe which expels a noisy and noxious trail of exhaust fumes.

For boys the car is all of these things: a unique symbol of self. For girls this usually is much less so, although it can serve a like purpose for those who have not yet fully accepted their female identity. For the girl who accepts her femaleness, though, the boy friend's car becomes a kind of extension of him. It is an object of admiration serving her new feelings for the male which have replaced her earlier feelings of envy.

Finally and importantly, the automobile brings the boy and girl together away from adults. It provides privacy for sexual experimentation, and ultimately serves the seeking and attaining of sexual identity and the establishment of mature heterosexual relationships.

THE RESOLUTION OF ADOLESCENCE

Ideally, the resolution of adolescence is characterized by: (1) the attainment of separation and independence from the parents; (2) the establishment of sexual identity; (3) the commitment to work; (4) the development of a personal moral value system; (5) the capacity for lasting relationships and for both tender and genital sexual love in heterosexual relationships; and (6) a return to the parents in a new relationship based upon a relative equality.

The adolescent joins the adult world with an ability and a motivation to come to terms with it, although not always accepting the same values as were prescribed by the preceding generations. The new orientations toward self, the adult world, and life are made possible by the achievement of independence and the establishment of a firm identity, and by the re-establishment of adequate ways of dealing with the instinctual drives so as to maintain a relatively stable mental and emotional equilibrium.

No matter how disturbed adolescents may seem or in fact are, the possibility for successful functioning in adulthood is good, so long as their adaptive and defensive mechanisms remain flexible and there is hope for a healthy resolution. Once the various conflicts are resolved, whether by healthy or pathologic means, adolescence has come to an end.

❦ 4

Dynamics of Adult Responses to Adolescence

Because of the rapid physical growth and the striking physiological changes of puberty and the associated changes in personality and behavior, adolescence coerces attention. Adults recognize that the adolescent, verging as he does on the attainment of full physical and sexual maturity, must be reckoned with by society. He and his peers constitute the next available creative and productive resources of his cultural group. With his great energy, increasing freedom from parental supervision, and eagerness for and accessibility to new ideas and ideologies, he carries a tremendous constructive or destructive potential.

As was stated, adults seem to have repressed the feelings and conflicts of their own adolescent years and therefore find it difficult to draw upon them to identify with the adolescent and understand his dilemma sufficiently to be helpful to him. The adolescent, just by being and behaving, stirs up anxiety, consternation, and alarm in parents and adults generally. Attempts to solve disputes and conflicts by discussion and reason often fail, and the adult then either gives up in despair or reverts to the use of his waning authority. As a result, the adolescent and the adult tend to become alienated from each other, and the adolescent tends to feel that he is being managed and pushed around rather than respected as an individual with rights of his own.

The cultural institutions relating to adolescence can be viewed as the defensive response of adults to adolescents. One determinant of

95

these adult (societal) responses is the set of expectations, conscious or unconscious, regarding the role or roles the adolescent is to fulfill in society. It seems reasonable to assume that these expected roles generally are designed to fit in with and bolster the existing culture. Youngsters are expected to be patriotic and willing to fight for their country. They are expected to be religious, to attend church, and maybe to teach Sunday school. If they work, they should help support the household. If they go to school, they can at least baby-sit for younger siblings and do chores. Should they marry, they are expected to choose partners who will better the social and economic status of the family. Their career choice, too, should fit into family and cultural expectations.

On the one hand, adults are interested in maintaining the status quo because their identity and security lie in the known and existing culture; a major effort directed toward adolescents is aimed at preserving the existing mores and cultural institutions. On the other hand, individuals and cultures both may at times run counter to this generalization. Adults who are open-minded and farsighted will want their children to become mature and press for healthy and constructive cultural change. In cultures undergoing major transitions, such as our own, adults unfortunately may not agree on basic moral values and social principles. How late, for example, should a 15-year-old come home from a date? The answer is as variable as the individual family. The nature of adult expectations or, indeed, the confusion or absence of consistent expectations, is determined by such uncertainty.

The consistency or inconsistency of cultural attitudes has important bearing upon the emotional health of the young person. It has been suggested that children do not become neurotic because of culturally determined frustrations but because the culture is unclear or in conflict as to the value of the imposed frustrations. For example, it is easier to adapt to premarital sexual abstinence when the sacredness of marriage and the inevitability of divine punishment for sin are a real and meaningful part of the cultural beliefs. An attitude that lacks firmness, both in individual adults and in the culture, fails to provide a definitive model for either identification or rebellion. A further reduction in the clarity of role expectations derives from the loss of clear differentiation of male and female roles in the family and in society.

Certain of the expectations thrust upon the future adults may be seen both as a projection of the adult's needs upon the adolescent and as the adult's defense against self-disruption. The adolescent becomes an extension of the adult, with the imposed burden of maintaining and fulfilling the wishes of the adult. The classic example is the parent who, lacking the opportunity or the talent to achieve some highly valued goal such as attaining a college education, then urges this goal upon his youngster. Such a parent urgently wants his own feelings of failure and inadequacy to be undone through the achievements of his children.

Adult reaction to adolescence also is determined by the presence of unresolved unconscious conflicts in the individual parent and family. Such conflicts may interfere with the parents' double-edged task of interpreting and presenting cultural values to the adolescent, while allowing him the freedom needed for the formation of individual identity. The overstrictness of some parents in trying to curb any sexual experience in their adolescent offspring can paradoxically be accompanied by seductive, sexually stimulating parental behavior which excites the very emotions the parent is at such pains to proscribe. Unconscious parental wishes are expressing one attitude while their conscious directives are saying the exact opposite.

For example, a father may share the bathroom with his teenage daughter in the morning when they both are clad only in undergarments; and he may forbid his daughter to join her friends at a party that evening because he has heard that they tell dirty jokes in mixed company. The girl receives a contradictory and confusing message which is further confused because she knows that most fathers don't share the bathroom with their teenage daughters, and also that other fathers are not so strict and forbidding or seemingly sure that boys and girls are out to do "bad" things. Thus the personal conflicts and defenses of the parents may make them poor conveyors of the culturally prescribed attitudes.

The adult expectations of adolescents, then, may reflect unresolved problems in the adult. Besides attempting to shift responsibility upon the adolescent, demanding that he accomplish something or uphold values that the adult himself has evaded, some adults may unconsciously "parentify" the adolescent out of a wish to reverse the existing order and be dependent upon and learn from him. Other adults may unconsciously perceive the child as a kind of extension of themselves, thus entirely obscuring the adolescent's strivings for identity.

The adolescent not only runs afoul of unresolved parental conflicts but often is uniquely provocative and effective in arousing such conflicts out of repression and into activity. This is a major factor in the widespread intolerance so many adults feel regarding adolescents. The aggressive and sexual behavior of the adolescent may stir up a variety of feelings in the adult. Middle-class parents coming home at night and finding their teenage son in an erotic tangle with the neighbor's daughter may respond by "not seeing" what is going on, by laughing over it, by delivering a lecture, or in certain "emancipated" settings by giving their approval.

The adolescent questioning of adult values and the refusal to accept the society's institutions on faith also create unpleasant feelings of doubt and anxiety in the adult, as well as a renewed awareness of their shortcomings and failures. Unsatisfying or inappropriate resolutions of sexual identity or of occupational and ideological choice are insecure at best. Some of the outmoded, ineffectual, or even harmful approaches to life upon which adults have based their lives may be mercilessly exposed by adolescent skepticism. For example, parents may have painfully evolved a precarious but workable balance among the strict religious attitudes of their own parents, the less conservative religious activities of their current social group, and their own personal doubts and convictions about religious issues; but this balance can be upset by the teenager's blunt challenges and "logical" criticisms of what the parents profess. The painful exposure and self-reappraisal caused by the "show me," "prove it" attitude of the adolescent and his behaving in ways that adults may envy but no longer allow themselves are difficult to experience with equanimity.

Another source of adult discomfort in their relationship with adolescents is the fact that the vigorous, healthy, attractive youngster can be an object of sexual interest to the parent, partly consciously and partly unconsciously. Parent-child attractions are not one-way responses, and their revival in adolescence can be quite strongly evocative of reciprocal parental desire. Such desire is as taboo for the parent as for the youngster, and normally is warded off. Adult intolerance and avoidance of adolescents often serve much the same defensive purposes as does the adolescent repudiation of the parents.

In this general context, it is important to note that parenthood may appropriately be considered a stage in human development. The defensive behavior of parents toward their children is determined by several factors: (1) the continued and dynamically significant existence in the parent (at conscious or unconscious levels or both) of unresolved conflicts from their own childhood experiences; (2) the omnipresent wish for solution of these conflicts in order to gain relief from tension; (3) the opportunity for attempt at solution by reliving one's own childhood vicariously through identification with the child.

Cultural institutions are the standardized and generally agreed upon means of both expressing and inhibiting instinctual drives. Cultural mores may be regarded as mass defensive-adaptive maneuvers aimed at achieving a workable compromise between universal biological drives and locally shared standards and values. Adolescents are gadflies on the body of culture, and in this role they have a therapeutic effect on adults, stimulating them to change; age inevitably yields to youth. It is at the boundary between adolescence and adulthood that cultural change and movement so often take place.

Conclusion

The normal adolescent has many tasks to achieve in progressing from childhood to adulthood. He simultaneously reappraises himself and his parents, but with less idealization and distortion and more reality testing than in earlier childhood. He sees his parents and himself as human beings with strengths and weaknesses. He makes new value judgments concerning those components of his identity which have been derived largely from his parents and which are internalized in his ego, his conscience, and his ideals. Hopefully, he retains the healthy identifications and discards the inappropriate or unrealistic ones, thereby attaining both an internal harmony and a workable relationship with society.

He comes to terms with the changes taking place in his body, experimenting with and mastering his new sexual and aggressive capacities. Simultaneously, he finds ways of controlling and harnessing the increased energy of his drives. He begins to reintegrate himself, establishing a new identity which includes modifications in his body image, a concept of himself as an emerging adult with the capacity for procreation, and a value system that he accepts as his own rather than as something imposed upon him by his parents. He looks to the future, making decisions about his education and occupation, recognizing these as prerequisites to his other major goal: the choosing of a marriage partner and having a family of his own.

As these various tasks are gradually accomplished, the adolescent relinquishes his attachment to the peer group and begins to form a new, more mature relationship with adults, including his parents,

CONCLUSION

which is characterized by respect and true "give and take," but also by the maintenance of his integrity, autonomy, and a realistic amount of independence. When he marries he ultimately is capable of loving his children and his mate, the latter both tenderly and sexually. In this new family he will seek fulfillment of normal dependency needs and, as a parent, will once again tend to relive and rework the conflicts of his own childhood and adolescence.

Several points of particular emphasis may be distilled from this book:

1. The reasonably stable equilibrium that marks the psychological offset of adolescence is one of dynamic tension, not stasis. It is likely to be breached by any of a variety of crises in the future: the normal physiological crises such as pregnancy, menopause, and senility; the normal human crises such as marriage, having children, illness, and death; and the crises of fate such as fire, flood, or loss of job.

2. The specific form and manifestations of adolescence are the result of the continuous interaction of biological, cultural, and psychological forces. The surge of puberty imparts particular urgency to the interplay of these forces. In our culture this is a time of crisis, often of great crisis. In other cultures puberty may cause little disturbance in the current of life.

3. A surprising number of cultural customs and institutions may be understood as resulting from the reactions of adults to adolescents. They evolve in response to the challenge which adolescents present to the adult society with its existing cultural values and mores.

4. The conflict between the generations can be an enriching experience to a society, and it often is the nodal point for cultural change. Change may occur on either side of the interface between the generations; adolescents, especially late adolescents, introduce much that is new; and adults can respond with new attitudes and solutions. Commonly, however, there is a derogation of adolescents—an understandable defensive reaction on the part of the adults who feel that they are being displaced.

We return inevitably to a contemplation of the nature of the culture within which this exciting and distinctively human phase of development occurs. Despite the universality of puberty the response which it compels in our middle-class culture is unique, and would be unintelligible in any other culture.

In this book we have attempted to delineate adolescence, not to judge it. It is a fact, however, that adolescents are constantly being judged by our culture. Adolescence is a difficult time for both youngsters and society, and it is only appropriate that any evaluative questions be directed both ways. In a rapidly moving and complex culture such as ours parental models may at times be inapplicable or inadequate. Parents may often be misguided in the styles of personality they wish to impose upon their children, and the adolescent often must improvise his identity as he goes along.

Through what customs and institutions can society best compensate for the shortcomings of individual parents? How useful are the stereotyped styles of adolescent rebellion to the individual seeking an identity? How does resisting authority train one to bear it? How can the fear of excessive dependency and loss of identity be reconciled with the wish to be loved and to belong? To what degree is one a potential beneficiary of society, and to what degree is society one's enemy? How far can one go in changing himself, and to what extent can one change society?

Our perspective brings home to us the possibility not only of disturbances in adolescent development but also of consistent pathogenic social norms in our culture. Our culture is only one of many cultures, a blindly made human creation out of the past, a phenomenon we might be better able to control if we understood it and to revise if we knew what was needed. To a degree, every society manufactures its own problems and, in ours, an example may be the "problem" of adolescence. Preventive psychiatry looks beyond a knowledge of causes to effecting a change in epidemiological conditions. Therapy of cultural institutions would appear to be as much of a possibility and a need as is the therapy of individuals.

Free communication between adolescent and adult is difficult, so much so that many professional observers doubt that the differences between the generations in a rapidly moving society can be bridged. They feel that perhaps the most that can be hoped for is mutual tolerance, sincere negotiation, and relatively peaceful coexistence. We

CONCLUSION

who formulated this report accept the difficulty, even the improbability, of achieving truly empathic relationships between successive generations. Nevertheless, we hope that this comprehensive presentation of the dynamic interaction of biological, psychological, and cultural forces in the adolescent stage of development will help provide understanding and perspective, promote mutual tolerance, and facilitate more realistic and constructive relationships between adolescents and adults.

Appendix A[1]

It is beyond the scope of this book to present a complete discussion of pubertal anatomy and physiology, but some of the details and statistics of development are included here.

Endocrinology of Adolescence

There is general agreement among endocrinologists that the events of the adolescent growth spurt take place under hormonal control. Normal maturation depends upon the orderly development and functioning of the hypothalamic-pituitary-gonadal-adrenal mechanism. The time of puberty is one of great transition in which the activities of the hypothalamic-pituitary mechanism change from those governing somatic growth and development alone to those regulating also the secretion of sex hormones. There occurs a complex series of changes in glandular secretion rates and possibly in the responsiveness of various tissues to the hormones.

The timing of adolescent sexual development appears to depend primarily on the maturation of certain centers in the central nervous system. It is thought that this removes some nerve cell inhibition and the anterior pituitary is stimulated, possibly through the formation of a "gonadotropin-releasing factor" in the hypothalamus. Puberty is initiated by pituitary gonadotropic activity, as is indicated by the ap-

[1] This statement relies heavily on the publications of Tanner, Wilkins, Talbot, et al., and Heald, et al. For further information the reader is referred to their work and the work of others given in the Bibliography.

pearance of urinary gonadotropins, with the production of follicle-stimulating hormone (in both sexes) and luteinizing hormone (female) or interstitial-cell-stimulation hormone (male).

Urinary gonadotropins are not usually demonstrable in the male before the age of 13 years when their appearance is coincident with growth of testes and scrotum. Follicle-stimulating hormone is responsible for the development of the semeniferous tubules and for spermatogenesis. Interstitial-cell-stimulating hormone causes differentiation of the interstitial tissue into Leydig cells which secrete androgens, the principal one being testosterone. It is necessary for the testes to be in the scrotum for spermatogenesis to occur. In cryptorchidism the testes remain within the abdominal cavity and the spermatic cells in the tubules do not mature, although androgen is produced and virilization takes place. The incidence of undescended testes is about 10 per cent at birth, with spontaneous descent reducing this figure to 3 per cent at 1 year of age and 0.3 per cent at puberty.

In the female, gonadotropins are first detected at the age of 11 years. Under the influence of follicle-stimulating hormone Graafian follicles in the ovaries begin to mature and to secrete estrogen. Luteinizing hormone is necessary to produce rupture of the follicle and discharge of the mature ovum. The corpus luteum forms rapidly and under the further influence of luteinizing hormone secretes progesterone. Progesterone causes the secretory changes in the endometrium of the uterus and lobular-acinar changes in the breasts during the luteal phase of the menstrual cycle. With fluctuating and increasing release of gonadotropins from the pituitary, the ovarian endocrine activity increases in cyclic fashion until menarche occurs at age 12 or 13. During early adolescence menstrual periods frequently occur in response to hormonal fluctuation without ovulation taking place.

During the preadolescent years in both sexes estrogen and androgen are formed in small amounts by the adrenal glands. Estrogen is found in very low quantities in the urine of both boys and girls from 3 to 8 years of age. In both sexes there is a slow rise until age 11, which in the male continues through maturation. In the female, with production of estrogen by the ovary, there is a pronounced rise which increases until about three years after menarche.

ENDOCRINOLOGY OF ADOLESCENCE

Estrogen stimulates early puberty fat deposition in both sexes. In girls this continues in characteristic distribution such as on breasts, hips, and legs. In the male, estrogen may cause transient mammary tissue development. In the female, estrogen is responsible for the growth and development of the nipple and duct structures of the breasts and of the labia minora, vulva, vagina, uterus, and fallopian tubes. The vaginal epithelium changes to stratified squamous type, and preparations of vaginal smears can be examined in order to reveal the presence and extent of estrogen activity.

Adrenal androgens, detected by the urinary excretion of neutral 17-ketosteroids, are formed in small and gradually increasing amount in both sexes from birth to 9 years. At 9 years, there is a more rapid increase in urinary 17-ketosteroids which is similar in males and females until about 15 years of age. With the onset of testicular function, there is an additional increase in 17-ketosteroids which eventually makes the excretion in males 20 per cent to 50 per cent greater than in females. This rise slowly continues after adolescence until a maximum is attained in the young adult.

The sex hormones, probably acting synergistically with growth hormones, are responsible for the adolescent growth spurt, with the greater increase in boys being due to the production of testosterone by the testes. The average annual linear growth in both sexes changes from two inches to three inches at age 10 to 11 in girls and age 14 to 15 in boys. During the growth spurt the epiphyseal centers in bones enlarge and epiphyseal lines gradually narrow until fusion occurs and growth stops.

In boys, the shoulders and thoracic cage broaden. In girls, there is the characteristic broadening of the pelvis. In boys, there is a rapid increase in weight with a heavy increase in musculature.

In both sexes, androgens are responsible for the appearance and sequential changes of pubic and axillary hair and for the development of sweat and sebaceous glands. In males, androgens cause increase in the vascularity, circumference, and length of the penis and growth and pigmentation of scrotal skin, which is wrinkled by the development and action of the dartos muscle. Androgens cause growth of the prostate gland and seminal vesicles and also the development of facial hair and larynx with deepening of the voice. In the female, androgens are responsible for the development of the labia majora and clitoris, the analogs of the scrotum and penis.

Sequence of Pubertal Phenomena

In girls the onset of the phenomena of puberty takes the following order: initial enlargement of the breasts; appearance of straight, pigmented pubic hair; maximum physical growth; appearance of kinky pubic hair; menstruation; growth of axillary hair. It is noteworthy that menstruation occurs after full growth has been attained, almost invariably after the apex of the growth in height. Full reproductive function follows the onset of menstruation by one or more years, and maximal fertility occurs in the early 20s.

In boys the corresponding order of pubescent phenomena is: beginning growth of the testes; straight, pigmented pubic hair; beginning enlargement of the penis; early voice changes; first ejaculation; kinky pubic hair; age of maximum growth; axillary hair; marked voice changes; and development of the beard. Rapid growth in height and in size of the penis normally occurs about a year after testicular development.

GENITAL DEVELOPMENT IN MALES

Stage 1. (Prepubertal.) Testes, scrotum, and penis are about the same size and proportion as in early childhood.

Stage 2. (Pubertal.) Enlargement of scrotum and testes. The skin of the scrotum reddens and changes in texture. Little or no enlargement of the penis at this stage.

Stage 3. Enlargement of the penis, mainly in length. Further growth of testes and scrotum.

Stage 4. Increased size of penis with growth in diameter and development of glans. Further enlargement of testes and scrotum; increased darkening of scrotal skin.

Stage 5. Genitalia adult in size and shape.

SECONDARY SEX CHARACTERISTICS

The average age span for these changes is 12 to 16 years; the normal age limits within which the changes may occur is 10 to 18 years.

Development of Secondary Sex Characteristics

BREAST CHANGES

Stage 1. (Prepubertal.) Elevation of papilla only.
Stage 2. (Pubertal.) Breast bud stage: elevation of breast and papilla as a small mound. Enlargement of areolar diameter.
Stage 3. Further enlargement of breast and areola, with no separation of their contours.
Stage 4. Projection of areola and papilla to form a secondary mound above the level of the breast.
Stage 5. Mature stage: projection of papilla only, due to recession of the areola to the general contour of the breast.

The average age span of these changes is 11 to 13½ years; the normal age limits for appearance of the breast bud stage is 8 to 13 years. The development of glandular alveoli for lactation awaits the occurrence of pregnancy.

(The male breast areola usually doubles it diameter; in about one third of boys there is some mammary development and areolar projection.)

CHANGE OF VOICE

Voice changes in males are due to enlargement of the larynx, which usually takes place concurrently with growth of the penis; the voice begins to deepen perceptibly as the development of the penis nears completion. Voice deepening is often so gradual, however, that it is of little value for precise evaluation of pubertal development.

PUBIC HAIR

Stage 1. (Preadolescent.) No differentiation between hair over the pubes and over the abdominal wall.

Stage 2. Sparse growth of long, slightly pigmented downy hair, straight or only slightly curled, chiefly at the base of the penis or along the labia.

Stage 3. Considerably darker, coarser, and more curled hair, spread sparsely over the junction of the pubes.

Stage 4. Adult in type, but considerably smaller in area than adult. No spread to the inner surface of the thighs.

Stage 5. Adult in quantity and type with distribution of the horizontal pattern. Spread to inner surface of thighs, but not up the linea alba or elsewhere above the base of the inverse triangle.

Stage 6. Further spread of pubic hair in about 80 per cent of men and 10 per cent of women, but this stage often is not completed until the mid-20s or later.

The normal age limits for the occurrence of Stage 2 in girls is 8 to 14; the average age span for Stages 2 through 5 is 11 to 14 years. In boys, Stage 2 normally occurs within the age limits of 10 to 15 years; the average age span for Stages 2 through 5 is 12 to 16 years.

AXILLARY AND FACIAL HAIR

Axillary hair usually follows the appearance of pubic hair by about two years. The facial hair of boys grows simultaneously with the axillary hair. Typically, the first growth and pigmentation occur at the corners of the upper lip and then spread across the upper lip, to the upper part of the cheeks and in the midline below the lower lip, to the sides and lower border of the chin, and finally to the neck.

SWEAT AND SEBACEOUS GLANDS

In both boys and girls enlargement of the apocrine sweat glands, with the typical odor of perspiration, begins at about the time axillary hair starts to grow. At the same time the sebaceous glands enlarge and become more active. Because the secretory ducts of these glands do not enlarge proportionately to deal with the increased secretion, they often become plugged and are easily infected. The resulting condition is acne, a common and quite normal affliction characteristic of the adolescent stage.

Appendix B

Committees,* Members, and Officers of the GROUP FOR THE ADVANCEMENT OF PSYCHIATRY as of July 1, 1967

COMMITTEE ON AGING
Jack Weinberg, *Chmn.*, Chicago
Robert N. Butler, Washington, D.C.
Alvin I. Goldfarb, New York
Lawrence F. Greenleigh, Los Angeles
Maurice E. Linden, Philadelphia
Prescott W. Thompson, Topeka
Montague Ullman, Brooklyn

COMMITTEE ON CHILD PSYCHIATRY
Suzanne T. van Amerongen, *Chmn.*, Boston
E. James Anthony, St. Louis
H. Donald Dunton, New York
John F. Kenward, Chicago
William S. Langford, New York
Dane G. Prugh, Denver
Exie E. Welsch, New York

COMMITTEE ON COLLEGE STUDENT
Harrison P. Eddy, *Chmn.*, New York
Robert L. Arnstein, New Haven
Alfred Flarsheim, Chicago

Alan Frank, Boulder, Colo.
Malkah Tolpin Notman, Brookline, Mass.
Earle Silber, Washington, D.C.
Benson R. Snyder, Cambridge, Mass.
Tom G. Stauffer, Scarsdale, N.Y.
J. B. Wheelwright, San Francisco

COMMITTEE ON THE FAMILY
Israel Zwerling, *Chmn.*, New York
Ivan Boszormenyi-Nagy, Philadelphia
L. Murray Bowen, Chevy Chase, Md.
David Mendell, Houston
Norman L. Paul, Cambridge, Mass.
Joseph Satten, Topeka
Kurt O. Schlesinger, San Francisco
John P. Spiegel, Cambridge, Mass.
Lyman C. Wynne, Bethesda, Md.

COMMITTEE ON
GOVERNMENTAL AGENCIES
Harold Rosen, *Chmn.*, Baltimore
William H. Anderson, Lansing, Mich.

* The members of the Committee on Adolescence are listed in the Preface on page 10.

Calvin S. Drayer, Philadelphia
Edward O. Harper, Cleveland
John E. Nardini, Washington, D.C.
Donald B. Peterson, Fulton, Mo.
Robert L. Williams, Gainesville, Fla.

COMMITTEE ON
INTERNATIONAL RELATIONS
Robert L. Leopold, *Chmn.,* Philadelphia
Francis F. Barnes, Chevy Chase, Md.
Joseph T. English, Washington, D.C.
Louis C. English, Pomona, N.Y.
John A. P. Millet, New York
Bertram Schaffner, New York
Mottram P. Torre, New Orleans
Bryant M. Wedge, Princeton, N.J.

COMMITTEE ON MEDICAL EDUCATION
David R. Hawkins, *Chmn.,* Chapel Hill, N.C.
Hugh T. Carmichael, Chicago
Robert S. Daniels, Chicago
Raymond Feldman, Boulder, Colo.
Saul Harrison, Ann Arbor
Herbert C. Modlin, Topeka
William L. Peltz, Philadelphia
David S. Sanders, Beverly Hills
Roy M. Whitman, Cincinnati

COMMITTEE ON
MENTAL HEALTH SERVICES
Lucy D. Ozarin, *Chmn.,* Bethesda, Md.
Walter E. Barton, Washington, D.C.
Morris E. Chafetz, Boston
Merrill Eaton, Omaha
James B. Funkhouser, Richmond, Va.
Robert S. Garber, Belle Mead, N.J.
Ernest W. Klatte, Talmage, Calif.
W. Walter Menninger, Topeka
Francis J. O'Neill, Central Islip, N.Y.
Lee G. Sewall, N. Little Rock, Ark.
Jack A. Wolford, Pittsburgh

COMMITTEE ON
MENTAL RETARDATION
Leo Madow, *Chmn.,* Philadelphia
Howard V. Bair, Parsons, Kans.
Peter W. Bowman, Pownal, Me.
Stuart M. Finch, Ann Arbor
Irving Philips, San Francisco
George Tarjan, Los Angeles
Warren T. Vaughan, Jr., San Mateo
Thomas G. Webster, Bethesda, Md.
Henry H. Work, Los Angeles

COMMITTEE ON
PREVENTIVE PSYCHIATRY
Stephen Fleck, *Chmn.,* New Haven
Gerald Caplan, Boston
Jules V. Coleman, New Haven
Leonard J. Duhl, Washington, D.C.
Albert J. Glass, Oklahoma City
Benjamin Jeffries, Harper Woods, Mich.
E. James Lieberman, Washington, D.C.
Mary E. Mercer, Nyack, N.Y.
Harris B. Peck, Bronx, N.Y.
Marvin E. Perkins, New York
Harold M. Visotsky, Chicago
Stanley F. Yolles, Chevy Chase, Md.

COMMITTEE ON
PSYCHIATRY AND LAW
Zigmond M. Lebensohn, *Chmn.,* Washington, D.C.
Edward T. Auer, St. Louis
John Donnelly, Hartford
Jay Katz, New Haven
Carl P. Malmquist, Minneapolis
Seymour Pollack, Los Angeles
Alan A. Stone, Cambridge, Mass.
Gene L. Usdin, New Orleans
Andrew S. Watson, Ann Arbor

APPENDIX B

COMMITTEE ON
PSYCHIATRY AND RELIGION
John W. Higgins, *Chmn.*, St. Louis
Sidney Furst, New York
Stanley A. Leavy, New Haven
Earl A. Loomis, Jr., New York
Albert J. Lubin, Woodside, Calif.
Mortimer Ostow, New York

COMMITTEE ON
PSYCHIATRY AND SOCIAL WORK
Edward C. Frank, *Chmn.*, Louisville
C. Knight Aldrich, Chicago
Maurice R. Friend, New York
John MacLeod, Cincinnati
John Nemiah, Boston
Eleanor A. Steele, Denver
Edward M. Weinshel, San Francisco

COMMITTEE ON
PSYCHIATRY IN INDUSTRY
Harry H. Wagenheim, *Chmn.*, Philadelphia
Spencer Bayles, Houston
Thomas L. Brannick, Rochester, Minn.
Matthew Brody, Brooklyn
Herbert L. Klemme, Topeka
Jeptha R. MacFarlane, Westbury, N.Y.
Alan A. McLean, New York
Kenneth J. Munden, Memphis
Clarence J. Rowe, St. Paul
Graham C. Taylor, Montreal, Canada

COMMITTEE ON PSYCHOPATHOLOGY
Milton Greenblatt, *Chmn.*, Boston
Wagner H. Bridger, New York
Neil R. Burch, Houston
James H. Ewing, Wallingford, Pa.
Daniel X. Freedman, Chicago
Paul E. Huston, Iowa City

P. Herbert Leiderman, Palo Alto, Calif.
George E. Ruff, Philadelphia
Charles Shagass, Philadelphia
Albert J. Silverman, New Brunswick, N.J.
Marvin Stein, Brooklyn

COMMITTEE ON PUBLIC EDUCATION
Peter A. Martin, *Chmn.*, Detroit
Leo H. Bartemeier, Baltimore
H. Waldo Bird, St. Louis
Lloyd C. Elam, Nashville
Dana L. Farnsworth, Cambridge, Mass.
John P. Lambert, Katonah, N.Y.
Mildred Mitchell-Bateman, Charleston, W. Va.
Mabel Ross, Boston
Mathew Ross, Chestnut Hill, Mass.
Julius Schreiber, Washington, D.C.
Kent A. Zimmerman, Berkeley

COMMITTEE ON RESEARCH
Morris A. Lipton, *Chmn.*, Chapel Hill, N.C.
Grete Bibring, Cambridge, Mass.
Louis A. Gottschalk, Cincinnati
Sheppard G. Kellam, Chicago
Gerald L. Klerman, New Haven
Ralph R. Notman, Brookline, Mass.
Franz Reichsman, Brooklyn
Richard E. Renneker, Los Angeles
Alfred H. Stanton, Boston

COMMITTEE ON SOCIAL ISSUES
Perry Ottenberg, *Chmn.*, Philadelphia
Viola W. Bernard, New York
Robert Coles, Cambridge, Mass.
Lester Grinspoon, Boston
Joel S. Handler, Chicago

Harold I. Lief, New Orleans
Judd Marmor, Los Angeles
Roy W. Menninger, Topeka
Arthur A. Miller, Chicago
Peter B. Neubauer, New York
Charles A. Pinderhughes, Boston

COMMITTEE ON THERAPEUTIC CARE
Benjamin Simon, *Chmn.*, Boston
Ian L. W. Clancey, Ottawa, Canada
Thomas E. Curtis, Chapel Hill, N.C.
Robert W. Gibson, Towson, Md.
Harold A. Greenberg, Bethesda, Md.
Henry U. Grunebaum, Boston
Bernard H. Hall, Topeka
Lester H. Rudy, Chicago
Melvin Sabshin, Chicago
Robert E. Switzer, Topeka

COMMITTEE ON THERAPY
Peter H. Knapp, *Chmn.*, Boston
Henry W. Brosin, Pittsburgh
Eugene Meyer, Baltimore
William C. Offenkrantz, Chicago
Lewis L. Robbins, Glen Oaks, N.Y.
Albert E. Scheflen, Bronx, N.Y.
Harley C. Shands, New York
Lucia E. Tower, Chicago

CONTRIBUTING MEMBERS
Marvin L. Adland, Chevy Chase, Md.
Carlos C. Alden, Jr., Williamsville, N.Y.
Kenneth E. Appel, Philadelphia
M. Royden C. Astley, Pittsburgh
Charlotte Babcock, Pittsburgh
Walter H. Baer, Peoria, Ill.
Grace Baker, New York
Benjamin H. Balser, New York
Bernard Bandler, Boston
Alfred Paul Bay, Topeka
Anna R. Benjamin, Chicago
A. E. Bennett, Berkeley
Robert E. Bennett, Princeton, N.J.

Ivan C. Berlien, Coral Gables, Fla.
Sidney Berman, Washington, D.C.
Edward G. Billings, Denver
Carl A. L. Binger, Cambridge, Mass.
Daniel Blain, Philadelphia
Wilfred Bloomberg, Hartford
C. H. Hardin Branch, Salt Lake City
Ewald W. Busse, Durham
Dale C. Cameron, Washington, D.C.
Norman Cameron, New Haven
Harvey H. Corman, New York
Frank J. Curran, New York
Bernard L. Diamond, Berkeley
Franklin G. Ebaugh, Denver
Stanley H. Eldred, Belmont, Mass.
Joel Elkes, Baltimore
O. Spurgeon English, Narberth, Pa.
Jack R. Ewalt, Boston
Lawrence Z. Freedman, Chicago
Thomas M. French, Chicago
Moses M. Frohlich, Ann Arbor
Daniel H. Funkenstein, Boston
George E. Gardner, Boston
J. S. Gottlieb, Detroit
Maurice H. Greenhill, Scarsdale, N.Y.
John H. Greist, Indianapolis
Roy R. Grinker, Chicago
Ernest M. Gruenberg, New York
David A. Hamburg, Palo Alto, Calif.
Herbert I. Harris, Cambridge, Mass.
Leonard E. Himler, Ann Arbor
J. Cotter Hirschberg, Topeka
Edward J. Hornick, New York
Roger William Howell, Ann Arbor
Joseph Hughes, Philadelphia
Portia Bell Hume, Berkeley
Robert W. Hyde, Boston
Lucie Jessner, Washington, D.C.
Irene M. Josselyn, Phoenix
Marion E. Kenworthy, New York
Edward J. Kollar, Los Angeles
Othilda Krug, Cincinnati

APPENDIX B

Lawrence S. Kubie, Sparks, Md.
Paul V. Lemkau, Baltimore
Maurice Levine, Cincinnati
David M. Levy, New York
Robert J. Lifton, Woodbridge, Conn.
Erich Lindemann, Palo Alto, Calif.
Hyman S. Lippman, St. Paul
Reginald S. Lourie, Washington, D.C.
Alfred O. Ludwig, Boston
LeRoy M. A. Maeder, Philadelphia
Sydney G. Margolin, Denver
Helen V. McLean, Chicago
Karl Menninger, Topeka
James G. Miller, Ann Arbor
Angel N. Miranda, Hato Rey, P.R.
Rudolph G. Novick, Des Plains, Ill.
Humphry F. Osmond, Princeton, N.J.
Eveoleen N. Rexford, Cambridge, Mass.
Milton Rosenbaum, New York
W. Donald Ross, Cincinnati
Elvin M. Semrad, Boston
William M. Shanahan, Denver
Benjamin M. Spock, New York
Edward Stainbrook, Los Angeles
Brandt F. Steele, Denver
Rutherford B. Stevens, New York
Lloyd J. Thompson, Chapel Hill, N.C.
Harvey J. Tompkins, New York
Arthur F. Valenstein, Cambridge, Mass.
Helen Stochen Wagenheim, Philadelphia
Raymond W. Waggoner, Ann Arbor
Robert S. Wallerstein, San Francisco

Cecil L. Wittson, Omaha
David Wright, Providence

LIFE MEMBERS
S. Spafford Ackerly, Louisville
Earl D. Bond, Philadelphia
John R. Rees, London, England
Bruce Robinson, Culver, Ind.
Francis H. Sleeper, Augusta, Me.

OFFICERS
President
Herbert C. Modlin
Box 829, Topeka, Kans. 66601
Vice President
John Donnelly
200 Retreat Avenue
Hartford, Conn. 06102
Secretary-Treasurer
Malcolm J. Farrell
Box C, Waverley, Mass. 02178
Asst. Secretary-Treasurer
Paul E. Huston
500 Newton Road
Iowa City, Iowa 52241

PUBLICATIONS BOARD
Chairman
Milton Greenblatt
15 Ashburton Place
Boston, Mass. 02108

Maurice R. Friend
Louis A. Gottschalk
Bernard H. Hall
John Nemiah
Perry Ottenberg
Henry H. Work

Bibliography

THE BIOLOGY OF ADOLESCENCE

AUSUBEL, DAVID P.: *Theory and Problems of Adolescent Development,* New York: Grune & Stratton, 1954.

BARTON, W. H., AND E. E. HUNT, JR.: "Somatotype and Adolescence in Boys: A Longitudinal Study," *Human Biology* 34: 254–270, Dec. 1962.

COHEN, Y.: *The Transition from Childhood to Adolescence,* Chicago: Aldine Publishing Company, 1964.

FRANK, L. K., AND ASSOCIATES: *Personality Development in Adolescent Girls.* Monograph of the Society for Research in Child Development, Inc., Vol. XVI, serial 53, 1951.

HALL, G. STANLEY: *Adolescence,* New York: Appleton, 1904.

HEALD, F. P., M. DANGELA, AND P. BRUNSCHUYLER: "Medical Progress— Physiology of Adolescence," *New England Journal of Medicine* 268, Jan.–June 1963.

KRIMS, B. M.: "Psychiatric Observations on Children with Precocious Physical Development," *Journal of the American Academy of Child Psychiatry* 1: 379–413, 1962.

MONTAGU, M. F. ASHLEY: *Adolescent Sterility,* Springfield, Ill.: Charles C Thomas, 1946.

MORE, D. M.: *Developmental Concordance and Discordance During Puberty and Early Adolescence.* Monograph of the Society for Research in Child Development, Inc., Vol. XVIII, serial 56, No. 1, 1953.

ROSENBAUM, M.: "The Role of Psychological Factors in Delayed Growth at Adolescence: A Case Report," *American Journal of Orthopsychiatry* 29: 762–771, 1959.

SHUTTLEWORTH, F. K.: *The Adolescent Period: A Graphic Atlas.* Monograph of the Society for Research in Child Development, Inc., Vol. XIV, serial 49, Nos. 1 and 2, 1949.

TALBOT, N. B., E. H. SOBEL, J. W. McARTHUR, AND J. D. CRAWFORD: *Functional Endocrinology from Birth through Adolescence,* Boston: Harvard University Press, 1952.

TANNER, J. M.: *Growth at Adolescence,* Springfield, Ill.: Charles C Thomas, 1962.

WILKINS, L.: *The Diagnosis and Treatment of Endocrine Disorders in Childhood and Adolescence,* 3rd edition, Springfield, Ill.: Charles C Thomas, 1965.

YOUNG, W. C. (editor): *Sex and Internal Secretion,* 3rd edition, Baltimore: Williams & Wilkins, 1961.

CULTURE AND ADOLESCENCE

ARIÈS, PHILIPPE: *Centuries of Childhood, A Social History of Family Life,* New York: Vintage Books, 1965.

BENEDICT, RUTH: *Patterns of Culture,* Boston: Houghton Mifflin, 1934, pp. 130–172.

———: "Sex in Primitive Society," *American Journal of Orthopsychiatry,* 9 (1939) 570–574.

COHEN, Y.: *The Transition from Childhood to Adolescence,* Chicago: Aldine Publishing Company, 1964.

GROUP FOR THE ADVANCEMENT OF PSYCHIATRY, Committee on the College Student: *Sex and the College Student,* New York: Atheneum, 1966.

HANDY, E. S. C.: "Native Culture of the Marquesas," *Bulletin of the Bishop Museum,* Honolulu, 9 (1923), 36–40.

HARING, DOUGLAS G. (editor): *Personal Character and Cultural Milieu,* Syracuse University Press, 1956.

HENRY, JULES: *Culture Against Man,* New York: Random House, 1963.

HILL, W. W.: "Note on the Pima Berdache," *American Anthropologist* 40 (1938), 338–340.

KAPLAN, BERT (editor): *Studying Personality Cross-Culturally,* Evanston, Ill.: Row, Peterson, 1961.

LA BARRE, WESTON: *The Human Animal,* University of Chicago Press (Phoenix Books), 1954.

LINTON, RALPH: *The Study of Man,* New York: Appleton-Century, 1936, p. 480.

LOWIE, ROBERT H.: *Primitive Religion,* New York: Boni & Liveright, 1924, pp. 181, 217, 243ff.

MACOBY, ELEANOR E. (editor): *The Development of Sex Differences,* University of Stanford Press, 1966.

MEAD, MARGARET: "Contrasts and Comparisons from Primitive Society," in B. J. Stern (editor), *The Family Past and Present,* New York: Appleton Century, pp. 3–13.

BIBLIOGRAPHY

TAYLOR, G. RATTRAY: *Sex in History,* New York: Vanguard, 1954.

WESTERMARCK, EDWARD: *The History of Human Marriage,* 3 vols., London: Macmillan, 1925, iii, 133–141, 198–206.

PSYCHOLOGY OF ADOLESCENCE AND DYNAMICS OF ADULT RESPONSES TO ADOLESCENCE

ADATTO, C. P.: "Ego Reintegration Observed in Analysis of Late Adolescents," *International Journal of Psychoanalysis,* Vol. XXXIX, 1958; p. 172.

AICHHORN, A.: *Wayward Youth,* New York: Viking, 1948.

BERNFELD, S.: "Types of Adolescence," *Psychoanalytic Quarterly,* Vol. VII, 1938; p. 243.

BLOS, P.: "The Contribution of Psychoanalysis to the Treatment of Adolescents," in *Psychoanalysis and Social Work.* (M. Heiman, editor), New York: International Universities Press, 1953.

———: "Preadolescent Drive Organization," *Journal of the American Psychoanalytic Association,* Vol. VI, 1958; p. 47.

———: *On Adolescence, A Psychoanalytic Interpretation,* New York: The Free Press of Glencoe, 1962.

BORNSTEIN, B.: "Masturbation in the Latency Period," *Psychoanalytic Study of the Child,* Vol. VI, New York: International Universities Press, 1951.

———: "On Latency," *Psychoanalytic Study of the Child.* Vol. VIII, New York: International Universities Press, 1953.

BRUCH, H.: "Psychological Aspects of Obesity in Adolescence," *American Journal of Public Health,* Vol. 48, 1958; pp. 1349–1353.

DEUTSCH, H.: *The Psychology of Women. I.,* New York: Grune & Stratton, 1944.

ERIKSON, E. H.: "The Problems of Ego Identity," *Journal of the American Psychoanalytic Association,* Vol. 4, pp. 56–121, 1956.

———: *Childhood and Society.* New York: Norton, 1950, 2nd ed., Norton paperback, 1963.

———: "Identity and the Life Cycle," *Psychological Issues,* Vol. 1, No. 1, New York: International Universities Press, 1959.

FRAIBERG, S.: "Some Considerations in the Introduction to Therapy in Puberty," *Psychoanalytic Study of the Child,* Vol. X, p. 264, 1955.

FREUD, A.: "Adolescence," *Psychoanalytic Study of the Child,* Vol. XIII, New York: International Universities Press, 1958.

———: *The Ego and the Mechanisms of Defense,* New York: International Universities Press, 1946.

———: *Normality and Pathology in Childhood Development,* New York: International Universities Press, 1965.

FREUD, S.: *The Ego and the Id*, standard edition, Vol. XIXI. London: Hogarth Press, 1961.

———: *Three Essays on the Theory of Sexuality*, standard edition, Vol. VII, London: Hogarth Press, 1953.

———: *The Passing of the Oedipus-Complex*, Collected Papers, Vol. II, London: Hogarth Press, 1949.

GARDNER, G. E.: "Psychiatric Problems of Adolescence," in *American Handbook of Psychiatry*, (S. Arieti, Editor), New York: Basic Books, 1959.

GELEERD, E. R.: "Some Aspects of Ego Vicissitudes in Adolescence," *Journal of the American Psychoanalytic Association*, Vol. 9, 1961; pp. 394–405.

GITELSON, M.: "Character Synthesis: The Psychotherapeutic Problem of Adolescence," *American Journal of Orthopsychiatry*, Vol. 18, 1948; pp. 422–431.

GREENACRE, P.: "The Prepuberty Trauma in Girls," in *Trauma, Growth and Personality*. New York: Norton, 1952.

GROUP FOR THE ADVANCEMENT OF PSYCHIATRY, Committee on the College Student: *Sex and the College Student*, New York: Atheneum, 1966.

HALL, G. STANLEY: *Adolescence*, New York: Appleton, 1904.

HARTMANN, H.: "Ego Psychology and the Problem of Adaptation," New York: International Universities Press, 1959.

INHELDER, B., AND J. PIAGET: *The Growth of Logical Thinking*, New York: Basic Books, 1958.

JACOBZINER, H.: "Attempted Suicides in Adolescence," *Journal of the American Medical Association*, 191 (1), 1965; pp. 101–105.

JONES, E.: "Some Problems of Adolescence," *Papers on Psychoanalysis*, 5th edition, London: Bailliere, Tindall, & Cox, 1949; p. 389.

JOSSELYN, I. M.: *The Adolescent and His World*, New York: Family Service Association of America, 1952.

———: "The Ego in Adolescence," *American Journal of Orthopsychiatry*, Vol. XXIV, 1954.

LAMPL-DE GROOT, J.: "On Masturbation and Its Influence on General Development," Vol. V., *Psychoanalytic Study of the Child*, 1950; p. 153.

MICHAELS, J. J.: "Character Disorders and Acting Upon Impulse," In: *Readings in Psychoanalytic Psychology*, (M. Levitt, Editor), New York: Appleton-Century-Crofts, 1958.

PEARSON, G. J. J.: *Adolescence and the Conflict of Generations*, New York: Norton, 1958.

PIAGET, J.: *The Growth of Logical Thinking from Childhood to Adolescence*, New York: Basic Books, 1958.

SCIENTIFIC PROCEEDINGS: Panel Reports. "The Psychology of Adolescence," *Journal of the American Psychoanalytic Association*, Vol. 6, pp. 111–120.

BIBLIOGRAPHY

Shapiro, R. L.: "Adolescence and the Psychology of the Ego," *Psychiatry* 26: 77–87, 1963.

Solnit, A. J.: "The Vicissitudes of Ego Development in Adolescence," panel report, *Journal of the American Psychoanalytic Association,* Vol. VII, 1959.

Spiegel, L. A.: "A Review of Contributions to a Psychoanalytic Theory of Adolescence," *Psychoanalytic Study of the Child,* Vol. VI, p. 375.

————: "Comments on the Psychoanalytic Psychology of Adolescence," *Psychoanalytic Study of the Child,* Vol. XIII, p. 296.

Wittels, F.: "The Ego of Adolescents," in: *Searchlights on Delinquency* (K. R. Eissler, editor), New York: International Universities Press, 1949.

Index

Accidents among adolescents, 25
Acne, 24, 109
Action, impulsive behavior and, 75–76
Adult prerogatives, attainment of, 91
Adulthood
  criteria of, 28–29
  discontinuity of role from childhood to, 44–48
  functional, 28–29
    in Western culture, 32, 33–34
  status of, 29
    among Mentawei, 30
    among Nayar, 30
    in Negro Africa, 37
    among Polynesians, 31
    in Western culture, 32–33, 34
Adults
  adolescents' relationships with, 67–68
  attitudes toward adolescents by, 7, 95–99
Africa, adult status in, 37
Aggressive drives, 25–26, 35–36
  dancing and, 69–70
  during early adolescence, 65, 78–79
  during latency stage, 54
  middle-class morality and, 43

Alienation, 82
American Indians, see Indians
American middle class, 38–44
Anal intercourse, 77
Anxiety
  in adolescents, 24–25, 75
  castration, 52, 71, 72
Appalachian personality, 38
Appetite, preadolescent increase of, 58
Asceticism, 25
Automobile, importance of, 92–93
Axillary hair, 109

Bar mitzvah ceremony, 36, 37
Berdache ("not-man"), among Plains Indians, 35–36
Biology of adolescence, see Puberty
Bisexuality in puberty, 24
Body image, development of, 74–75, 79
Borneo
  head-hunting in, 36
  "sleep-crawling" in, 31–32
Boys
  development of body image in, 74–75
  first phase of adolescence in, 59–60
  growth rate of, 21–22

latency stage in, 54–55
masturbation in, 25, 55–56, 57,
 70–73, 77
oedipal phase in, 52, 53
preadolescence in, 57, 58
puberty in, 65
 sequence of, 107
relationship with girls, 77–78
symbolism of automobile to, 93
Breast changes, 108

Car, importance of, 92–93
Castration anxiety, 52, 71, 72
Childhood
 discontinuity of role from, 44–48
 experience of, 51–55
Christian culture, aggressive drives
 in, 35
Ciscisbei, 30, 31
Coitus during adolescence, 37,
 85–88
College age, adolescents at, 81
Conformity, individuality versus, 41
"Crushes" on adults, 67
Cryptorchidism, 105
Cultural facilitation, inhibition
 and, 35–38
Cultural factors, 27–49, 95–96, 99
 American middle class, 38–44
 criteria for adulthood, 28–29
 cultural facilitation and
  inhibition, 35–38
 discontinuity of role from
  childhood to adulthood,
  44–48
 environment, 29–32
  Western culture as, 32–34
 rapid social change, 48–49
 universal tasks, 34–35

Dancing, 69–70
Dating, earliest phases of, 78–79

Death, major cause of adolescent, 25
Dobuans (Melanesia), "sleep-
 crawling" among, 31
Drinking, adolescent, 92

Education, demand for more, 46–47
Ego, 50
 in early adolescence, 64–65
 at offset of adolescence, 62
 power shift from id to, 60–61
Ejaculation, 64, 71, 73
Endocrinology, *see* Hormonal
 activity
Environment, 29–32
 Western culture as, 32–34
Ethics, decreasing adherence to
 Judaeo-Christian, 45
Existential philosophy, 48

Facial hair, 109
Facilitation, *see* Cultural facilitation
Family of procreation, definition
 of, 29
Family of origin, definition of, 29
Fellatio, 77
Functional adulthood, 28–29
 in Western culture, 32, 33–34

Genitalia
 development of male, 107
 See also Penis; Testes
Germany, Hitler "ideal" in, 89
Girls
 breast changes in, 108
 development of body image in,
  74–75
 growth rate of, 21–22
 latency stage in, 54–55
 masturbation in, 25, 70–73, 77
 menstruation in
  discussion of, 55, 56
  onset of, 23, 59, 64, 73–74, 105

oedipal phase in, 52, 53
preadolescence in, 57–58
relationships with boys, 77–78
sequence of pubertal phenomena
    in, 107
symbolism of automobile to, 93
Grading systems, emphasis of, 46
Grooming, adolescents' interest
    in, 24
Growth spurt, pubertal, 21–22

Hair
    axillary and facial, 109
    pubic, 108–9
Head-hunting, 35, 36
Hiatus status of adolescents, 40
High school age, adolescents at, 81
Hitler "ideal," 89
Homosexual behavior during early
    adolescence, 77
Hormonal activity
    preadolescent, 58
    in puberty, 20–21, 24, 104–7
Human nature, learning of, 19

Id, 50
    domination by ego and superego
        of, 62–63
    power shift to ego from, 60–61
Idealism in late adolescence, 88–90
Identity, 47–48
    adult prerogatives and, 92
    idealism and, 88–90
    occupational choice and, 90–91
Impulsive behavior, 25, 75–76
Incest taboo, 34, 64
Independence, move toward, 65–68
Indians (American)
    aggressive drives among Plains,
        35–36
    role training among Papago, 45
Individuality versus conformity, 41

Indonesia
    adult-status "maturity" among
        Mentawei of, 30
    head-hunting in, 35
Inhibition, cultural facilitation
    and, 35–38
Intellectualization as adolescent
    defense, 25–26

Jewish bar mitzvah ceremony, 36, 37
Judaeo-Christian ethics, decreasing
    adherence to, 45

Kahioi, 31
Kinship family, definition of, 29
Klinefelter's syndrome, 22n.

Latency stage, 53–55, 66
Love, adolescent
    coitus and, 85–88
    idealism and, 89

Malabar, status of social fatherhood
    among Nayar of, 30, 31
Masturbation, 25, 55–56, 57, 70–
    73, 77
Melanesia
    "sleep-crawling" among Dobuans
        of, 31
    head-hunting in, 35
Mentawei (Indonesia), adult-status
    "maturity" among, 30
Menstruation
    discussion of, 55, 56
    onset of, 23, 59, 64, 73–74, 105
Middle class, American, 38–44
Morality, middle-class, 42–44
Mourning about withdrawal from
    parents, 66–67

Nambutiri Brahmans (Malabar),
    31
National temperament, 29

Nayar (Malabar), status of social fatherhood among, 30, 31
Negro Africa, adult status in, 37
Negro ghettos, individual "success" in, 38
New Guinea, head-hunting in, 36
Nonconformist, society's reaction toward, 83
Nuclear family
definition of, 29
middle-class organization around, 41–42, 43

Obesity in adolescents, 24
Occupational choice, identity and, 90–91
Oceania
emphasis on status in, 31
status displacement of father by maternal uncle in, 30
See also Melanesia
Oedipal phase, 52–53
Oral-genital contact (fellatio), 77
Ordeals, puberty, 36
Orgasm
adolescent experiments with, 72–73
capacity for, 64

Papago Indians, role training among, 45
Parents
late adolescence and, 84, 92
move toward independence from, 65–68, 79
responses to adolescents by, 97–99
sexual feelings toward, 64–65
Peer groups
adolescent, 39, 68–70, 79
preadolescent, 56–57
Penis
automobile as symbol of, 93
child's curiosity about, 51–52
size of, 23, 71
Physical activity, increase in preadolescence of, 58
Plains Indians, aggressive drives among, 35–36
Play, sense of, 82–83
Polynesians, sexual and status maturity among, 31
Preadolescence, 55–58
Premarital sex, 37, 85–88
"Professional" adolescents, 40
Promiscuity, 25
Protracted adolescence, 63
Psychological aspects of puberty, 24–26
Psychology of adolescence, 50–94
beginning and ending of adolescence, 59–63
early adolescence, 63–90
late adolescence, 80–94
preadolescence and, 55–58
role of childhood experience in, 51–55
Puberty, 59, 63, 101–2
changes of, 20–22
endocrinology of, 20–21, 24, 104–7
impact of, 64–65
psychological and social aspects of, 24–26
response of adolescents to, 22–24
sequence of phenomena in, 107–9
Puberty ordeal, 36
Pubic hair, 108–9

Reality, feeling in late adolescence toward, 82–83
Rites de passage, for adolescents, 37–38

INDEX

Roles, discontinuity from childhood to adulthood of, 44–48

Samoa, freedom from stress in, 36, 37
Sebaceous glands, 109
Self image, development of, 74–75, 79
Sex characteristics
  primary, 23
  secondary, 23–24, 64, 108–9
Sexual-functioning maturity, among Polynesians, 31
Sexual drives, 25–26
  dancing and, 69–70
  during early adolescence, 64–65, 77–79
  during latency stage, 54
  middle-class morality and, 42–44
  during preadolescence, 55–57
  in Samoa, 36
Sexual identity, 48, 53
Sexual intercourse during adolescence, 37, 85–88
"Sleep-crawling," 31–32
Social aspects of puberty, 24–26
Social change, problem of rapid, 48–49
Society
  definition of, 27
  differences between child and adult and, 29–30
  late adolescence and, 80–83
Southern rural whites, 38
Status adulthood, 29
  among Mentawei, 30
  among Nayar, 30
  in Negro Africa, 37

among Polynesians, 31
in Western culture, 32–33, 34
Stealing, 25
Superego, 50, 64
  at offset of adolescence, 62
Sweat glands, 109

Taboos, incest, 34, 64
Tasks, universal adolescent, 34–35
Technology, demands of increasing, 46–47
Teenager, as term, 39
Telephoning, among adolescents, 69
Testes, incidence of undescended, 105
Thought, capacity for, 76–77
"Togetherness," 47
Tomboys, 57, 59
Turner's syndrome, 22n.

Universal tasks of adolescence, 34–35
Uterine brotherhood, definition of, 29

Virginity, 36–37, 42
Voice, change of, 108

Wa states, head-hunting in, 36
Wellington, Duke of, 75
Western culture
  as environment, 32–34
  Puritan heritage of, 85

Y-chromosome, maturation and, 22n.